God's Spiritual Prescriptions
For Healing, Liberation and Salvation

by
Willie James Webb

Copyright © 2001 by Willie James Webb
All rights reserved.
No part of this book may be reproduced, stored in a retrieval system, or transmitted by any means, electronic, mechanical, photocopying, recording, or otherwise, without written permission from the author.

ISBN: 0-75962-474-7

This book is printed on acid free paper.

1stBooks – rev. 7/10/01

Contents

FOREWARD		v
Introduction		vii
Chapter 1	The Framed Word	1
Chapter 2	Corrosive Spiritual Illness	6
Chapter 3	Spiritual Knowledge	30
Chapter 4	Spiritual Truth	36
Chapter 5	Spiritual Mandates	42
Chapter 6	Spiritual Rebellion	48
Chapter 7	Spiritual Counsel	55
Chapter 8	Spiritual Guidance	60
Chapter 9	Spiritual Appeal	67
Chapter 10	Spiritual Power	76
Chapter 11	Spiritual Deliverance and Restoration	84
Chapter 12	Spiritual Affirmation	89
Chapter 13	Spiritual Rewards	93
Chapter 14	Spiritual Salvation	101
Chapter 15	Frames and Prescriptions of Inspiration and Truth	108
Chapter 16	Strategy For The Publication of God's Word	180
General Modes for Publicizing God's Word		183

FOREWARD

This book has evolved over a period of three and a half decades of serious Bible study. It is the culmination of decades of teaching Sunday school, Bible classes, preparation and preaching sermons and reading scripture lessons from the pulpit. For a period of twenty years at the Wheat Street Baptist Church in Atlanta, Georgia, and for four years at the Foundation Baptist Church in Atlanta, I made preparations to read the scripture, pray and preach each Sunday with very few exceptions. This gave me an opportunity to become spiritually attuned with many scriptures in the Bible.

I had the good fortune of being introduced to the Bible as a youth. One of my earliest recollections as a preschool age child was being in church at a revival meeting with my mother in a small rural township in Alabama. It was my mother who taught me to kneel and pray along with her by the bedside at night. It was my oldest sister who started reading the Bible to me at about the age of five or six. During my elementary school years, I had the good fortune of walking about a mile and a half to Sunday school each Sunday with a young man by the name of Frank Crittenden who was about six years older than I. Frank became the Superintendent of the Sunday school and I started teaching a Sunday school class as a teenager.

Additionally, during my adolescent and early adulthood years, I had about seven summers of very enriching religious exposures in a Boardwalk Chapel in Wildwood, New Jersey. I lived and worked in a summer resort hotel about three blocks from the Boardwalk Chapel along the Atlantic Ocean. This Chapel, operated by the Presbyterian Church was open seven days a week with many trained ministers who preached, taught and showed many religious and scientific films. I also attended a Billy Graham Crusade in New York City during these summers.

The Boardwalk Chapel experience was significant and valuable for me for a number of reasons. I was from the rural racially segregated south and most of the pastors and preachers of my church did not have a high school education. They all were Black. At the Boardwalk Chapel, all of the ministers were White and seminary trained. In their Witness for Christ, they utilized films and other audio-visual equipment. They also displayed and sold many books and other religious literature. The seven summers that I spent in Wildwood, New Jersey, contributed greatly to my early Christian education and my appreciation for the beauty and power of scriptures.

It was at Morehouse College in Atlanta where I started my formal education for the ministry. In addition to receiving an undergraduate degree in Sociology and Religion, Morehouse College offered and required daily Chapel for all students. The daily Chapel for four years at Morehouse College was a most enriching, inspirational and educational experience. I was blessed with the teaching, preaching, singing and messages from well prepared educators, including scholarly, Dr. Benjamin E. Mays, who was president of Morehouse College for 27 years.

Upon graduation from Morehouse College, I received the M.A. Degree from Atlanta University and the M.S. Degree from Georgia State University 6 years later. This is the general background that I took into the professional world of work in Criminal Justice for twelve years, Mental Health for sixteen years and Substance Abuse Counseling and Education for seven years along with the commensurate continuing education.

I returned to academics and completed the Master of Divinity Degree from the Interdenominational Theological Center at the Morehouse School of Religion May 13, 2000. I am indebted to many of the professors at I.T.C. and also the staff at St. Luke Counseling and Training Center, where I completed my residency in clinical pastoral education by working with the Homeless people in Atlanta. I am also indebted to the many clients and students that I have worked with for the past 36 years), as well as staff members.

I am indebted to many people, relatives and friends in the production of this book. I am indebted especially to my wife, Wilma, and daughter, Karen, who offered not only their constructive criticism, but also allowed me time and space to write and compile this volume. Overall and through all it is the Holy Spirit.

I have been a student of life and religion as far back as I can remember. I cannot think of any experience that did not contribute to this book. My own personal trials and adversities also contributed significantly. As one who is a part of fallen humanity, a sinner saved by Grace, I have experienced over and over again, God's compassion, mercy, grace, forgiveness, healing, deliverance and restoration. His Word has been and is my Light, my Guide, my Comforter, my Hope and my Salvation. I have never experienced nor witnessed any human feeling or human situation where there was not a current relevant correlation in the Scriptures. This is the primary basis of *God's Spiritual Prescriptions*.

During my journeys through the Word of God from Genesis through Revelation, I have seen my failures, weaknesses and sins along with the rest of humanity. However, and most significantly, I have also seen the love of God, my Redeemer, my Lord and my Savior. It is my hope and my prayer that millions of others will experience this revelation through *God's Spiritual Prescriptions*.

Introduction

> Write the vision and make it
> plain upon tables, that he
> may run that readeth it.
> Habakkuk 2:2

The purpose of this book is to obey the vision to Habakkuk and to get the Word of God visibly and audibly published, pervasively, in the physical, social and spiritual environment of the human inhabitants of the earth. The Word of God must be regularly seen in our environment and surroundings. It must be regularly heard in our social environment, the homes, the churches, the schools, institutions, businesses, community and government. It, the Word of God, must be made available to be read, recited, sung, studied, discussed and practiced. Yes, there are millions of Bibles and other religious volumes in churches, homes, libraries, hotels and other establishments. But inspite of these millions of Bibles and other religious volumes, for the most part, the Word of God is hidden between the covers of the book in solitary and isolated places. The Word must be written upon tables and made plain so that he that sits, reclines, walks, runs, rides or flies, may be able to see it, read it, hear it and practice it.

The vision of Habakkuk has not been taken seriously. This is evident by our general society. The Word of God is difficult to be found in our society. Outside of the brief periods when it is read in churches, Bible classes and individual private readings, the visible and audible Word of God is almost non existent in our society. Habakkuk mandates that the vision be made plain upon tables. He suggests that it be made so plain that a person who is running can read it. Habakkuk is suggesting an enlargement of God's word out of the printed page and into the open environment for public consumption.

When we do a Bible count we can come up with very large numbers in the millions. However, when we look for the Word of God in the open environment, it is almost non existent, with a few rare exceptions. As we drive up and down the highways and as we walk the streets, we rarely see an open display of God's word. When we observe buildings in our cities and suburbs, we do not see the Word of God, not even on our churches. When we go inside of buildings, homes and churches included, rarely do we see the Word of God. You can take the trains, planes, motor vehicles or other modes of transportation from coast to coast in America, and rarely will you see the Word of God. Unread Bibles and unpublicized words of God do not help the cause of salvation.

> But if our Gospel be hid, it is hid
> to them that are lost.
> II Corinthian 4:3

We as custodians of God's word, are hiding, concealing, confining and limiting the Word of God by our failure to make it plain upon tables so that he that runs may read it. We, as Christians, are content to open our Bibles perhaps several times during the week. And so often we do not publicly share what we have read privately. We are not getting the Word of God from the printed page into the open environment. It is not enough to read the word to ourselves and keep it private. When we keep God's word to ourselves, are we not hiding the Word? Do we sense a responsibility to get the Word of God out into the public domain? Are there not some tables on which we can make the Gospel plain? Is there not a marketplace for God's word? Are we hiding the Gospel from them who are lost? Buried treasures, hidden talents and unsown seeds do not reap benefits or bear fruit.

Tragically, the Word of God has become a well kept secret. Although the Bible is well known. It is printed in more languages than any other book. It outsells all other books. We carry Bibles. We store and shelve them. We carry them to Bible class and church. The Bible encloses the word. As long as the word is enclosed, it is a concealed secret. God does not intend for his word to be a secret. The vital, life giving word of God, contained in the Bible, must be translated from hidden enclosures to open disclosures and public exposure. The purpose of this book is to provide the methods of publicizing the Word of God and also the vital messages for that publication. It was Habakkuk who saw the vision for exposing the Word of God in a bold and graphic way.

There were three distinct things in conjunction with the Holy Spirit that compelled the writing of this book. The first compelling reason was the inscription of a biblical quotation at the top of a school building in Wildwood, New Jersey. The concrete engraved inscription at the top of the multi-story Wildwood High School building, always fascinated me. Invariably, when passing by this building I would gaze up at the words from Proverbs 4:13, "Take fast hold of knowledge.. It is thy life." The concrete engravement was big and bold. It would be difficult for anyone to pass by, either by walking or riding, and fail to see this conspicuous proverbial inscription.

The second compelling reason contributing to the writing of this book was an inscription that I saw on a dollar bill. This dollar bill was among several that I received as change after paying for service on my automobile. The dollar bill had two words stamped on it in blue — JESUS SAVES. Through spiritual discernment, I immediately saw the connection and the meaning of the vision of Habakkuk. There is a need and commandment to make God's words plain upon tables so that he who walks, runs, rides or flies may read it.

The third reason for writing this book is based on the belief that the Word of God and only the Word of God is sufficient to save humanity and human culture from self destruction. It is believed that if the Word of God can be made sufficiently plain in the public domain, the growing secularistic destructive tide can be reversed. It is further believed that there is a special divine and spiritual power in the undiluted Word of God.

Core scriptures have been selected to concentrate the power of the word upon the most critical problems in the history of mankind. These scriptures have been selected under the guidance of the Holy Spirit. Many of these scriptures are based on my twenty years of experience in reading the scripture from the pulpit of the Wheat Street Baptist Church in Atlanta, Georgia. The unique method of this book is to let God's Word speak for Itself. The message to the witnesses of God - is to make the Word of God plain. The power is in the inspired Word of God. This is not a book of exegesis or hermaneutics that involves explaining and interpreting scripture. The scriptures speak for themselves. Each frame of scripture contains a significant message directly from the inspired Word of God.

The framed Word of God is the uniqueness of this book. Each page is a frame. Some of the pages contain four frames. And many of the frames contain just one or two sentences. The purpose and design of the frames are to make the word plain. The frames are designed so that the words can be inscribed on tables, walls, billboards, buildings or any other appropriate place. The frames contain the messages that can redeem, transform and revolutionize the world. It would not be practical to write a book or a chapter on a wall, because one who is in motion can only read a brief inscription. The frames are brief, and yet, powerful inspired Words of God. Consider the power in the words of Jesus when he told Nicodemus, "ye must be born again." Or when he gave a new commandment to his disciples, "Love one another as I have loved you."

I want to acknowledge my indebtedness to the late Reverend Lucius M. Tobin, my religion professor at Morehouse College. Rev. Tobin expressed the keenest insight than anyone I have ever known into the culture crisis of our time. His keen, inquisitive and penetrating mind was always analyzing beneath the surface and the superficial to the depth and breadth of every subject that impacted on human life. Rev. Tobin expressed consistently, that, if religion is to be relevant, it must incorporate social salvation and it must address the culture crisis. **God's Spiritual Prescriptions** is an effort to address our culture crisis. I pay tribute to the late illustrative Pastor of the Wheat Street Baptist Church in Atlanta, Ga. Rev. William H. Borders, Sr., who entrusted me as a pulpit associate minister for over twenty years to select and read the Scripture, teach and preach the Gospel with independence.

This book has an invaluable and inexhaustible use for the Christian practitioner and for all persons who value truth, sound doctrine and the accumulated wisdom of the ages. It is an inspiration for every true Believer. It can be used in every worship, spiritual and educational setting. It is ideal for meditations, devotions, sermons, seminars and forums. The organized scriptural orientation of this book around basic relevant themes, makes it a valuable book for many courses in Bible Colleges and Theological Seminaries.

This book is specifically designed for the pastoral counselor, trained spiritual and Christian Counselors. There is a specific frame or several frames that relate to each presenting issue in pastoral care and counseling. For the convenience of the counselor and spiritual practitioner, each frame has a reference number.

The reference number enables the counselor or skilled spiritual helper to use scripture in an appropriate, systematic, therapeutic and helpful manner.

The Bible is special revelation from God. It speaks to humanity. It speaks to nations, governments and all races of people. It speaks to every individual. Its message is all personal and corporate. It speaks to you and me. It addresses humanity's deepest, most vital and enduring needs. It describes our identification, our spiritual condition, our actions, directions, purpose, our relationship with each other and God. It describes our destiny. This message can be ignored and denied. However, it cannot be successfully and indefinitely evaded without dire and tragic consequences.

It is hoped that *God's Spiritual Prescriptions* will accelerate Bible study and make the scriptures more relevant to human needs in our time. Because the Bible is filled with infinite messages, it is not sufficient to just give someone a Bible to read. We can be more helpful as a reference in guiding their selection to the most relevant scriptures that meets their most urgent needs in their personal unique situations. Large libraries contain immeasurable volumes of information. Reference desks in libraries are available to assist prospective consumers in finding the desired information. Drug stores have designated sections for certain medications. They have trained licensed pharmacists to fill prescriptions. Should not the most important informational document of humanity be more accessible, systematized and referenced for practical human utilization? This book is an effort to begin that process.

Finally, there were many significant things in my early child-hood that shaped my world view. I was born into a loving Christian family and community in rural Notasulga (Macon County), Alabama. This was a time and place where nature was alive with singing birds, grazing cattle, waterbrooks, budding plants, blooming flowers, moonlit nights starry skies with the sound of crickets and the hooting owls in the still of the night. It was the time when we heard the play and laughter of children and the fun filled activities of adults. The singing, the humming and melodic whistling of cheery souls overshadowed the poverty in which we lived. We had much to be proud of in Macon County where Booker T. Washington founded Tuskegee Institute. This is the County where I experienced being reborned at the Macedonia Baptist Church in Notasulga. when I was a senior at Tuskegee Institute High School. These were the foundation experiences that propelled me through life in search of *God's Spiritual Prescriptions: For-Healing, Liberation and Salvation.*

Chapter 1

The Framed Word

A frame is the enclosure of something that is considered precious and treasured. A frame is used to enclose something beautiful and special. It is used for pictures, certificates and other items of significance. The frame is used in an effort to capture the beauty or preserve the significance of an object. In addition, to enclosing and preserving an object of significance, the frame is also used to put the significant object on display to be seen.

The pages in this book contain the framed Word of God. Every frame, whether one sentence or one page, has a significant message. Every message is suitable for placing on a wall or some conspicuous place to be observed. The message of each frame is an advantageous method of learning basic lessons and biblical truths without being confused or overwhelmed with multiple ideas and thoughts. The framed message is simple and direct. It is a more precise prescription. It eliminates the need to do a lot of searching for a specific biblical text. The framed message makes it possible to apply the Word of God objectively and relevantly to the respective need or issue.

The framed message allows the reader, observer or pastoral practitioner to focus on a central idea. A central idea can be more easily understood, digested and applied. There is a need to take prime time in reading, studying, sharing and personally understanding the inexhaustible truths of the Bible. This can be done best by explaining one basic thought at a time. This method allows time to meditate on the word and to internalize it.

The framed messages of this book represents a primary core meaning. It represents the heart of the matter or the meat of the substance. The framed word is like freeing the corn from the stalk, the husks and the cob. The stalk and the husks are coverings for the corn, but they are not the corn. The aim and the focus of this book is to get beyond the treasure chest to the treasure itself. It is to get beyond the wrappings to the gift. It is to get beyond the book and the pages to the message.

God's Spiritual Prescriptions is an effort to put God's Word on tables of display. It is an expression of an urgent need to unbag the seeds of life and sow them bountifully. Unwrap the gift and deliver it to the intended recipients. Unearth the treasure. Uncover the golden nuggets and share them liberally and boldly.

All scripture quoted in this book are taken from the Authorized King James Version of the Holy Bible.

GOD'S WORD

Thy word is a lamp unto my feet and a light unto my path.

   Psalm 119:105

Blessed are they that hear the Word of God, and keep it.

   Luke 11:28

My Word that goeth forth out of my mouth shall not return unto me void.

   Isaiah 55: 11

These words, which I command thee this day, shall be in thy heart, and thou shalt teach them diligently to thy children.

   Deuteronomy 6:6-7

From a child thou hast known the holy scriptures, which are able to make thee wise unto salvation.

   II Timothy 3:15

GOD'S WORD

Oh how I love thy law! It is my mediation all the day.

Psalm 119:97

I hope in thy Word.

Psalm 119:81

I trust in thy Word.

Psalm 119:42

I rejoice at thy Word.

Psalm 119:162

I have esteemed the Words of his mouth more than my necessary food.

Job 23:12

His word was in mine heart as a burning fire shut up in my bones, and I was weary with forbearing, and I could not stay.

Jeremiah 20:9

GOD'S WORD

The Word of our God shall stand forever.

Isaiah 40:8

The seed is the Word of God.

Luke 8:11

The sower soweth the Word of God.

Mark 4:14

My mother, and my brethren, are those who hear the Word of God, and do it.

Luke 8:21

If ye continue in my Word, then are ye my disciples indeed, and ye shall know the truth and the truth shall make you free.

John 8:31,32

All scripture is given by inspiration of God, and is profitable for doctrine, for reproof, for correction, for instruction in righteousness.

II Timothy 3:16

GOD'S WORD

In the beginning was the Word, and the Word was with God, and the Word was God.

   John 1:1

O Earth, Earth, Earth, hear the Word of the Lord.

   Jeremiah 22:29

Hear O Heavens, and give ear, O Earth; for the Lord hath spoken.

   Isaiah 1:2

Heaven and earth shall pass away, but my word shall not pass away.

   Luke 21:33

The Word of our God is quick and powerful, and sharper than any two edge sword.

   Hebrews 4:12

Entrance of thy Word giveth light.

   Palm 119:130

Chapter 2

Corrosive Spiritual Illness

Why is the moral fabric of our society deteriorating and degenerating at such a rapid and frightening rate? It is no mystery. It is no secret. There are evident and clearly identifiable reasons for this moral decline in our society. Not only can the causes be identified, the causes of moral decay are also preventable. The answers and solutions to the destructive problems of our society are available. Our failure to acknowledge the root causes of our moral decay and our refusal to apply the available solutions is an ongoing human tragedy.

Our problems are as old as mankind. Our solutions and answers have been available since creation. This chapter on corrosive spiritual illness is God's diagnosis of our problems and our debilitating illness. This chapter enumerates the spiritual illnesses of mankind and the present spiritual illnesses of the American society. The other chapters in this book provide the medicine, answers and solutions to the decompensating illness in the American society and the world.

The following enumerations identify our individual and corporate illness and the root cause of our social, economic, cultural, racial and political problems.

CORROSIVE SPIRITUAL ILLNESS

Attempts to Reduce the Truth to Relatavism

Woe unto them that call evil good, and good evil; that put darkness for light, and light for darkness; that put bitter for sweet, and sweet for bitter!

Isaiah 5:20

Woe unto them that are wise in their own eyes, and prudent in their own sight!

Isaiah 5:21

Ye shall not do after all the things that we do here this day, every man whatsoever is right in his own eyes.

Deuteronomy 12:8

CORROSIVE SPIRITUAL ILLNESS

Attempts to Reduce the Truth to Relatavism

Jesus saith unto him, I am the way, the truth and the life.

John 14:6

There is a way which seemeth right unto a man, but the end thereof are the ways of death.

Proverbs 16:25

For they being ignorant of God's righteousness, and going about to establish their own righteousness, have not submitted themselves unto the righteousness of God.

Romans 10:3

CORROSIVE SPIRITUAL ILLNESS

Crisis in Leadership

But when he saw the multitudes, he was moved with compassion on them, because they fainted, and were scattered abroad, as sheep having no shepherd.

Matthew 9:36

Woe be unto the pastors that destroy and scatter the sheep of my pasture! saith the Lord.

Jeremiah 23:1

Ye have scattered my flock, and driven them away, and have not visited them: behold, I will visit uypon you the evil of your doings, saith the Lord.

Jeremiah 23:2

CORROSIVE SPIRITUAL ILLNESS

Crisis in Leadership

Beware of false prophets, which come to you in sheep's clothing, but inwardly they are ravening wolves.

Matthew 7:15

The hireling fleeth, because he is an hireling, and careth not for the sheep.

John 10:13

Woe be the shepherds of Israel that do feed themselves! Should not the shepherds feed the flock!

Ezekiel 34:2

CORROSIVE SPIRITUAL ILLNESS

Crisis in Leadership

The diseased have ye not strengthened, neither have ye healed that which was sick, neither have ye bound up that which was broken, neither have ye brought again that which was driven away, neither have ye sought that which was lost; but with force and with cruelty have ye ruled them.

Ezekiel 34:4

As for my people, children are their oppressors, and women rule over them. O my people, they which lead thee cause thee to err, and destroy the way of thy paths.

Isaiah 3:12

There fore said he unto them, the harvest truly is great, but the labourers are few: pray ye therefore the Lord of the harvest, that he would send forth labourers into his harvest.

Luke 10:2

CORROSIVE SPIRITUAL ILLNESS

Failure To Acknowledge Jesus
As Lord and Saviour

In the beginning was the Word, and the Word was with God, and the Word was God. The same was in the beginning with God.

John 1:1-2

And the Word was made flesh, and dwelt among us, (and we beheld his glory, the glory as of the only begotten of the Father,) full of grace and truth.

John 1:14

Then spake Jesus again unto them, saying, I am the light of the world: he that followeth me shall not walk in darkness, but shall have the light of life.

John 8:12

CORROSIVE SPIRITUAL ILLNESS

*Failure To Acknowledge Jesus
As Lord and Saviour*

Wherefore God also hath highly exalted him, and given him a name which is above every name.: That at the name of Jesus every knee should bow, of things in heaven, and things in earth and things under the earth. And that every tongue should confess that Jesus Christ is Lord, to the glory of God the Father.

   Philippians 2:9-11

Neither is there salvation in any other: for there is none other name under heaven given among men, whereby we must be saved.

   Acts 4:12

Jesus saith unto him, I am the way, the truth, and the life: no man cometh unto the Father, but by me.

   John 14:6

CORROSIVE SPIRITUAL ILLNESS

Social Injustice

Now do ye Pharisees make clean the outside of the cup and the platter; but your in ward part is full of ravening and wickedness.

Luke 11:39

Woe unto you also, ye lawyers! for you lade men with burdens grievous to be borne, and ye yourselves touch not the burdens with one of your fingers. Woe unto you! for ye build the sepulchres of the prophets, and your fathers killed them.

Luke 11:46-47

He hath shewed thee, O man, what is good; and what doth the Lord require of thee, but to do justly, and to love mercy, and to walk humbly with thy God!

Micah 6:8

CORROSIVE SPIRITUAL ILLNESS

Social injustice

For ye have turned judgment into gall, and the fruit of righteousness into hemlock.

   Amos 6:12

Be not deceived, God is not mocked: For whatsoever a man soweth, that shall he also reap.

   Galatians 6:7

Hear this, O ye that swallow up the needy, even to make the poor of the land to fail.... I will turn your feasts into mourning, and all your songs into lamentation; and I will bring up sackcloth upon all loins, and baldness upon every head...and the end thereof as a bitter day.

   Amos 8:10

CORROSIVE SPIRITUAL ILLNESS

Ethnic Conflicts and Cultural Divesity

All we like sheep have gone astray; we have turned every one to his own way; and the Lord hath laid on him the iniquity of us all.

   Isaiah 53:6

And hath made of one blood all nations of men for to dwell on all the face of the earth, and hath determined the times before appointed, and the bounds of their habitation.

   Acts 17:26

There is one body, and one Spirit, even as ye are called in one hope of your calling, one Lord, one faith, one baptism, one God and Father of all, and in you all.

   Ephesians 4:4-6

CORROSIVE SPIRITUAL ILLNESS

Ethnic Conflicts and Cultural Diversity

Howbeit every nation made gods of their own, and put them in the houses of the high places which the Samaritans had made, every nation in their cities wherein they dwelt.

   II Kings 17:29

There is neither Jew nor Greek, there is neither bond nor free, there is neither male nor female: for ye are all one in Christ Jesus.

   Galatians 3:28

Now there are diversities of gifts, but the same Spirit. And there are differences of administrations, but the same Lord. And there are diversities of operations, but it is the same God which worketh all in all.

   I Corinthians 12:4-6

CORROSIVE SPIRITUAL ILLNESS

Greed

Labor not for the meat which perisheth, but for that meat which endureth unto everlasting life.

John 6:27

And I will say to my soul, soul, thou hast much goods laid up for many years; take thine ease, eat, drink and be merry. But God said unto him, thou fool, this night thy soul shall be required of thee: then whose shall those things be, which thou hast provided?

Luke 12:19-20

He that is greedy of gain troubleth his own house.

Proverbs 15:27

CORROSIVE SPIRITUAL ILLNESS

Greed

For the love of money is the root of all evil: which while some coveted after, they have erred from the faith, and pierced themselves through with many sorrows.

I Timothy 6:10

Yea, they are greedy dogs which can never have enough, and they are shepherds that cannot understand: they all look to their own way, everyone for his gain, from his quarter.

Isaiah 56:11

It is written, man shall not live by bread alone, but by every word that proceeded out of the mouth of God.

Matthew 4:4

CORROSIVE SPIRITUAL ILLNESS

Sensate Cultural Addictions

For they that sleep, sleep in the night; and they that be drunken are drunken in the night.

   I Thessalonians 5:7

Wherefore he saith, awake thou that sleepest, and arise from the dead, and Christ shall give thee light.

   Ephesians 5:14

Woe unto him that giveth his neighbor drink, that puttest thy bottle to him, and makest him drunken also, that thou mayest look on their nakedness!

   Habakkuk 2:15

CORROSIVE SPIRITUAL ILLNESS

Sensate Cultural Addictions

As it is written, the people sat down to eat and drink, and rose up to play.

   I Corinthians 10:7

Woe unto them that rise up early in the morning, that they may follow strong drink; that continue until night, till wine in flame them!

   Isaiah 5:11

And the harp, and the viol, the tabret, and pipe, and wine, are in their feasts: but they regard not the work of the Lord, neither consider the operations of his hands.

   Isaiah 5:12

CORROSIVE SPIRITUAL ILLNESS

False Religion

And why call ye me, Lord, Lord, and do not the things which I say?

Luke 6:46

I hate, I despise your feast days, and I will not smell in your solemn assemblies. Though ye offer me burnt offerings and your meat offerings, I will not accept them: Neither will I regard the peace offerings of your fat beasts.

Take thou away from me the noise of thy songs; for I will not hear the melody of thy viols.

But let judgment run down as waters, and righteousness as a mighty stream.

Amos 5:21-24

Be ye doers of the word and not hearers only, deceiving yourselves.

James 1:22

CORROSIVE SPIRITUAL ILLNESS

False Religions

But woe unto you, scribes and pharisees, hypocrites! for ye shut up the kingdom of heaven against men: for ye neither go in yourselves neither suffer ye them that are entering to go in.

   Matthew 23:13

And Jesus answering said, A certain man went down from Jerusalem to Jericho, and fell among thieves which stripped him of his raiment, and wounded him, and departed, leaving him half dead.

And by chance there came down a certain priest that way: and when he saw him, he passed by on the other side.

   Luke 10:30-31

But wilt thou know, O vain man, that faith without works is dead?

   James 2:20

CORROSIVE SPIRITUAL ILLNESS

The Proliferation of Unsound Doctrines

For other foundation can no man lay, than that is laid, which is Jesus Christ.

   I Corinthians 3:11

For the time will come when they will not endure sound doctrine: And they shall turn away their ears from the truth, and shall be turned unto fables.

   II Timothy 4:3,4

Now the Spirit speaketh expressly, that in the latter times some shall depart from the faith, giving heed to seducing spirits, and doctrines of devils.

   I Timothy 4:1

CORROSIVE SPIRITUAL ILLNESS

The Proliferation of Unsound Doctrines

Now I beseech you, brethren, mark them which cause divisions and offences contrary to the doctrine which ye have learned; and avoid them.

   Romans 16:17

Woe unto them that call evil good, and good evil; that put darkness for light, and light for darkness; that put bitter for sweet, and sweet for bitter!

   Isaiah 5:20

Hereby know ye the Spirit of God: Every spirit that confesseth that Jesus Christ is come in the flesh is of God. And every spirit that confesseth not that Jesus Christ is come in the flesh is not of God.

   I John 4:2-3

CORROSIVE SPIRITUAL ILLNESS

Secularistic Values and Sexual Carnality

Because that, when they knew God, they glorified him not as God, neither were thankful; but became vain in their imaginations, and their foolish heart was darkened. Professing themselves to be wise, they became fools.

Romans 1:21-22

Who changed the truth of God into a lie, and worshipped and served the creature more than the Creator, who is blessed forever. Amen.

Romans 1:25

For this cause God gave them unto vile affections: for even their women did change the natural use into that which is against nature: And likewise also the man, leaving the natural use of the woman, burned in their lust one toward another; men with men working that which is unseemly, and receiving in themselves that recompence of their error which was meet.

Romans 1:26-27

CORROSIVE SPIRITUAL ILLNESS

Secularstic Values and Sexual Carnality

God gave them over to a reprobate mind, to do those things which are not convenient.

   Romans 1:28

Being filled with all unrighteousness, fornication, wickedness, covetousness, maliciousness; full of envy, murder, debate, deceit, malignity; whisperers, backbiters, haters of God, despiteful, proud, boasters, inventors of evil things, disobedient to parents, without understanding, covenant breakers, without natural affection, implacable, unmerciful;

   Romans 1:29-31

Who knowing the judgment of God, that they which commit such things are worthy of death, not only do the same, but have pleasure in them that do them.

   Romans 1:32

CORROSIVE SPIRITUAL ILLNESS

The Transgression of God's Laws

The earth also is defiled under the inhabitants thereof; because they have transgressed the laws, changed the ordinance, broken the everlasting covenant.

   Isaiah 24:5

An sinful nation, a people laden with iniquity, a seed of evildoers, children that are corrupters: they have forsaken the Lord, they have provoked the Holy One of Israel unto anger, they are gone away backward.

   Isaiah 1:4

The whole head is sick, and the whole heart faint.... from the sole of the foot even unto the head thre is no soundness in it; but wounds, bruises and putrifying sores.

   Isaiah 1:5-6

CORROSIVE SPIRITUAL ILLNESS

The Transgression of God's Laws

For the wages of sin is death; but the gift of God is eternal life through Jesus Christ our Lord.

   Romans 6:23

Then when lust hath conceived, it bringeth forth sin: and sin, when it is finished, bringeth forth death.

   James 1:15

Think not that I am come to destroy the law, or the prophets: I am not come to destroy, but to fulfill.

   Matthew 5:17

Chapter 3

Spiritual Knowledge

Spiritual knowledge is the knowledge about the transcendent aspirations of humankind to relate to God and existence beyond the material world. It is knowledge about the innermost search of the soul for God, truth and purpose of life. It is a groping to understand the connections between the Creator and the creature, the divine and the human. Underneath it is man's search for God. From above, it is God's revelation and self-disclosure to mankind. The perception of this redemptive process is spiritual knowledge.

Spiritual knowledge is about a faith in God that enables or empowers a person to overcome the tragic predicament of sin, suffering and death. It is not faith of physical sight. It is a faith of spiritual insight. Spiritual knowledge is an understanding and a perception of God's love, purpose and destiny of man in and beyond history. This knowledge relates to man's vertical relationship to God and mankind's horizontal relationship with each other.

Spiritual knowledge is divine knowledge which informs man from above about God's will and ways. It is understanding of God's special revelation in the Bible and the glory of God as manifested in God's creation. It is knowledge about the ultimate purpose of human existence.

SPIRITUAL KNOWLEDGE

In the beginning God created the heaven and the earth.

    Genesis 1:1

The way of the ungodly shall perish.

    Psalm 1:6

The heavens declare the glory of God.

    Psalm 19:1

Man shall not live by bread alone.

    Matthew 4:4

SPIRITUAL KNOWLEDGE

The harvest truly is plenteous, but the labourers are few.

    Matthew 9:37

The wages of sin is death, but the gift of God is eternal life through Jesus Christ.

    Romans 6:23

The true worshippers shall worship the Father in Spirit and in truth.

    John 4:23

Faith cometh by hearing, and hearing by the word of God.

    Romans 10:17

SPIRITUAL KNOWLEDGE

For whatsoever a man soweth, that shall he also reap.

   Galatians 6:7

The love of money is the root of all evil.

   I Timothy 6:10

Ye are a chosen generation, a royal priesthood, an holy nation, a peculiar people.

   I Peter 2:9

Holy men of God spake as they were moved by the Holy Ghost.

   II Peter 1:21

SPIRITUAL KNOWLEDGE

The Lord knoweth how to deliver the godly out of temptations.

   II Peter 2:9

The day of the Lord will come as a thief in the night.

   II Peter 3:10

Love worketh no ill to his neighbor.

   Romans 13:10

Faith without works is dead.

   James 2:26

SPIRITUAL KNOWLEDGE

There is no fear in love, but perfect love casteth out fear.

I John 4:18

He that loveth not knoweth not God, for God is love.

I John 4:8

Chapter 4

Spiritual Truth

Spiritual truth is vital and critical for the escalating culture crisis that humanity faces in the New Millennium. In the midst of unprecedented social and technological changes and transitions in a dynamic globalizing world, what can be true and sound? How can absolutes exist in a relativistic world? How can commonalities be established in the midst of ethnocentric cultural diversity and religious pluralism? These questions make the truth and sound doctrine more difficult, and yet, more vital and urgent than ever before.

Fictions, fantasies and arbitrary decisions are unreliable and irresponsible as operational bases for the human corporate enterprise. Unsound doctrine and disregard for truth lead to unsound thinking, beliefs policies and actions. Ultimately, the disregard for truth and sound doctrine lead to chaos, social conflicts and human disasters

Spiritual truth is that stability in a higher reality which endures in the midst of change and transitions. Spiritual truth is a revelatory reality with an independent existence fixed by God. It is the core essence of itself Spiritual truth is light for the soul in the spiritual world, as the sun light for the eyes in the natural world. God's word is Light. Jesus is the legacy, guardian and personification of truth.

SPIRITUAL TRUTH

Man looketh on the outward appearance, but the Lord looketh on the heart.

   I Samuel 16:7

The earth is the Lord's and the fullness thereof, the world and they that dwell therein.

   Psalm 24:1

There is a way which seemeth right unto a man, but the end thereof are the ways of death.

   Proverbs 14:12

My people are destroyed for lack of knowledge.

   Hosea 4:6

SPIRITUAL TRUTH

The word was made flesh and dwelt among us.
  John 1:14

I am the resurrection and the life: he that believeth in me, though he were dead, yet shall he live.

  John 11:25

The world has hated them because they are not of the world.

  John 17:14

Then Peter opened his mouth and said, of a truth I perceive that God is no respecter of persons.

  Acts 10:34

SPIRITUAL TRUTH

He which soweth sparingly shall also reap sparingly.

   II Corinthians 9:6

There is neither Jew nor Greek, There is neither bond nor free, there is neither male nor female: for ye are all one in Christ Jesus.

   Galatians 3:28

Be not deceived. God is not mocked: for whatsoever a man soweth that shall he also reap.

   Galatians 6:7

God is light, and in him is no darkness at all.

   I John 1:5

SPIRITUAL TRUTH

The race is not to the swift nor the battle to the strong--Time and chance happens to them all.

   Ecclesiastes 9:11

All have sinned and come short of the glory of God.

   Romans 3:23

All things work together for good to them that love God.

   Romans 8:28

SPIRITUAL TRUTH

Some have entertained angels unawares.

   Hebrews 13:2

We love him because he first loved us.

   I John 4:19

The darkness is past and the true light now shineth.

   I John 2:8

He that doeth the will of God abideth forever.

   I John 2:17

Chapter 5

Spiritual Mandates

Spiritual mandates are authoritative scriptural laws, commands, instructions, prophetic and proverbial sayings based on the God inspired truth and wisdom of the ages. In addition to the Ten Commandments, the Bible has a multitude of other scriptural mandates in the Old and New Testaments. These mandates have strong messages of warnings, instructions, consequences, promises, help, comfort hope and love.

Spiritual mandates provide mankind with clear instructions on how to live a righteous and faithful life of priority and love. It teaches the right and proper relationships in human relations and relations with God. It warns of the negative consequences of disobedience and rewards obedience. These mandates teach us how to control our feelings and our actions in responsible constructive ways.

The authoritative spiritual mandates of the Bible is a complete roadmap for our lives. They teach us how to care about our personal, social, spiritual, communal, national and global lives. They teach us how to set priorities and live by the highest ethical and moral principals known to mankind.

If we learn, listen to and obey the mandates of scripture, our directions will be clearer; our purpose will be more noble; our burdens will be lighter; our world will be safer and we will be closer to the Kingdom of God.

SPIRITUAL MANDATES

Offer the sacrifices of righteousness and put your trust in God.

   Psalm 4:5

Trust in the Lord and do good.

   Psalm 37:3

Seek ye the Lord while he may be found, call ye upon him while he is near.

   Isaiah 55:6

Let Judgment run down as waters, and righteousness as a mighty stream.

   Amos 5:24

SPIRITUAL MANDATES

Let us lay aside every weight and the sin which doth so easily beset us, and let us run with patience the race that is set before us.

   Hebrews 12:1

Feed the flock of God which is among you.

   I Peter 5:2

Beloved, believe not every spirit, but try the spirits, whether they are of God.

   I John 4:1

Put on the whole armour of God, that ye may be able to stand against the wiles of the devil.

   Ephesians 6:11

SPIRITUAL MANDATES

Ye must be born again.

   John 3:7

Love one another as I have loved you.

   John 13:34

Feed my lambs. Feed My sheep.

   John 21:15-17

Ye shall receive power, after that the Holy Ghost is come upon you: and ye shall be witnesses unto me both in Jerusalem, and in all Judaea, and in Samaria, and unto the uttermost part of the earth.

   Acts 1:8

SPIRITUAL MANDATES

Call on the name of the Lord and be saved.

    Acts 2:21

Be not conformed to this world, but be ye transformed by the renewing of your mind.

    Romans 12:2

Walk in the spirit and ye shall not fulfill the lust of the flesh.

    Galatians 5:16

Be ye kind one to another, tenderhearted, forgiving one another, even as God, for Christ's sake, hath forgiven you.

    Ephesians 4:32

SPIRITUAL MANDATES

As ye have therefore received Christ Jesus the Lord, so, walk ye in him.

Colossians 2:6

Let the word of Christ dwell in you richly in all wisdom.

Colossians 3:16

Walk in wisdom toward them that are without, redeeming the times.

Colossians 4:5

Study to show thyself approved unto God, a workman that needeth not to be ashamed, rightly dividing the word of truth.

II Timothy 2:15

Chapter 6

Spiritual Rebellion

Spiritual rebellion is as old as mankind and it persists constantly in human nature. This rebellious spirit persists throughout history and to this present time, 2000 years after the coming of Christ. This rebellion is against the Creator and the moral order that God has prescribed for man to follow. To the extent that man rebels against the Creator, he rebels against himself and his own future interest. When man, the creature, knowingly and deliberately rebels against divine values, of goodness, righteousness, truth, beauty and justice, this is indicative of a humanly unfathomable spiritual defiance. What kind of spirit is it that would persist on initiating and participating in its own self destruction?

Spiritual rebellion represents a sick head and a sick heart. It cannot be isolated and studied in test tubes, under the microscope or with any other bio-technical means. However, it is real and lethal and must not be ignored. It must be acknowledged, studied and treated. The scriptures contain the diagnosis, prescription and remedy. Because of its infectious and progressive nature the remedy must be applied to avoid the demise of civilization.

The study of spiritual rebellion highlights the urgency and the importance of being transformed by the renewing of the mind, becoming a new creature and being born again.

SPIRITUAL REBELLION

Hast thou eaten of the tree, whereof I commanded thee thou shouldest not eat? And the man said, The woman whom thou gavest to be with me, she gave me of the tree, and I did eat.---and the woman said, the serpent beguiled me, and I did eat.

    Genesis 3:11-13

And God saw that the wickedness of man was great in the earth, and that every imagination of the thoughts of his heart was only evil continually.

    Genesis 6:5

And God looked upon the earth, and behold, it was corrupt; for all flesh had corrupted his way upon the earth.

    Genesis 6:12

And the Lord said in his heart, I will not again curse the ground any more for man's sake; for the imagination of man's heart is evil from his youth.

    Genesis 8:21

SPIRITUAL REBELLION

But this people hath a revolting and rebellious heart.

   Jeremiah 5:23

Your iniquities have turned away these things, and your sins have withholden good things from you.

   Jeremiah 5:25

But they rebelled and vexed his Holy Spirit.

   Isaiah 63:10

The whole head is sick, and the whole heart is faint. From the sole of the foot even unto the head there is no soundness in it; but wounds, and bruises, and petrifying sores.

   Isaiah 1:5-6

SPIRITUAL REBELLION

For we wrestle not against flesh and blood, but against principalities, against powers, against the rulers of the darkness of this world, against spiritual wickedness in high places.

   Ephesians 6:12

The thief cometh not, but for to steal, and to kill, and to destroy.

   John 10:10

Return ye, ye backsliding children, and I will heal your backsliding.

   Jeremiah 3:22

For as by one man's disobedience many were made sinners, so by the obedience of one shall many be made righteous.

   Romans 5:19

SPIRITUAL REBELLION

Now there was a day when the sons of God came to present themselves before the Lord, and Satan came also among them. And the Lord said unto Satan, whence comest thou? Then Satan answered the Lord and said, From going to and fro in the earth, and walking up and down in it.

Job 1:6-7

Again, the devil taketh him up into an exceeding high mountain, and sheweth him all the kingdoms of the world, and the glory of them. And saith unto him, All these things will I give thee, if thou wilt fall down and worship me.

Matthew 4:8-9

If the world hate you, ye know that it hated me before it hated you.

John 15:18

He came unto his own, and his own received him not.

John 1:11

SPIRITUAL REBELLION

For all have sinned and come short of the glory of God.

   Romans 3:23

All we like sheep have gone astray, we have turned everyone to his own way.

   Isaiah 53:6

For the good that I would I do not; but the evil which I would not, that I do.--- I find then a law, that, when I would do good, evil is present with me.

   Romans 7:19, 21

The people sat down to eat and drink and rose up to play.

   I Corinthians 10:7

SPIRITUAL REBELLION

For many deceivers are entered into the world, who confess not that Jesus Christ is come in the flesh. This is a deceiver and an antichrist.

II John 1:7

They shall turn away their ears from the truth.

II Timothy 4:4

For the time will come when they will not endure sound doctrine.

II Timothy 4:3

For they being ignorant of God's righteousness, and going about to establish their own righteousness, have not submitted themselves unto the righteousness of God.

Romans 10:3

Chapter 7

Spiritual Counsel

It is a common need of human beings at some point in their lives to be able to share their most perplexing thoughts and painful feelings. There is a need to relate to a congenial and compassionate significant other who is patient enough to listen, concerned enough to hear and cares enough to understand. The brokenhearted, the rejected, the captives and those who are bruised and discouraged are searching for spiritual counsel. Shared burdens are easier to bear. Externalized thoughts can be seen and understood more clearly when shared with a spiritual counselor.

The depressed and discouraged are often in need of someone to hear their story and consider the justification for their pain. In spiritual counsel, the counselee can be brought out of darkness into the light; from confusion to a new focus; from the depths of despair to the wings of new hope. New courage, increased faith, rearrangement of priorities, new dreams and visions can be realized through spiritual counsel.

It is not always easy to find a human spiritual counselor. The Scripture teaches that there is a wonderful counselor who cares about the broken hearted, the neglected, oppressed and abused. This Wonderful Counselor, Prince of Peace and Mighty God never slumbers nor sleeps. God's Grace is sufficient.

SPIRITUAL COUNSEL

And his name shall be called Wonderful Counselor.

   Isaiah 9:6

Consider and hear me, O Lord my God: Lighten mine eyes, lest I sleep the sleep of death.

   Psalm 13:3

Beware of false prophets

   Matthew 7:15

Recompense to no man evil for evil.

   Romans 12:17

SPIRITUAL COUNSEL

Thou shalt guide me with thy counsel, and afterward receive me to glory.

   Psalm 73:24

Where no counsel is the people fall: but in the multitude of counsellors there is safety.

   Proverbs 11:14

Come now, let us reason together saith the Lord.

   Isaiah 1:18

What doth the Lord require of thee, but to do Justly and to love mercy and to walk humbly with thy God?

   Micah 6:8

SPIRITUAL COUNSEL

Be not overcome of evil, But overcome evil with good.

   Romans 12:21

Let every soul be subject unto the higher powers.

   Romans 13:1

Render therefore to all their dues: tribute to whom tribute is due; custom to whom custom; fear to whom fear; honour to whom honour.

   Romans 13:7

Let this mind be in you that was also in Christ Jesus.

   Philippians 2:5

SPIRITUAL COUNSEL

Put on the whole armour of God.

Ephesians 6:11

Grow in grace and in the knowledge of our Lord and Savior Jesus Christ.

II Peter 3:18

Study to show thyself approved unto God rightly dividing the word of truth.

II Timothy 2:15

Therefore judge nothing before the time, until the Lord come, who both will bring to light the hidden things of darkness, and will make manifest the counsels of the hearts.

I Corinthians 4:5

Chapter 8

Spiritual Guidance

Life is a journey that can and does lead in many different directions, and to many different destinations. God created human beings with the freedom to choose and make independent decisions. Since there are destructive roads that lead to death, it is critical to have reliable guidance to travel the road that leads to life.

There are a multitude of false doctrines and unsound principals that can mislead. There are persons who mislead through pervasive deceptions. Some mislead through their own ignorance and darkness. We are capable of being mislead through our own pride, vanities, greed, impulsivity and self deceit.

As life becomes more and more complicated and perplexing, spiritual guidance from above is more vital and essential. Misguidance and loose cannons inevitably lead to chaos and disaster.

Spiritual guidance leads us out of darkness into the light, and from blindness and ignorance to knowledge and sight. It leads us away from conflict and confusion to cooperation and peace. It leads us from hopelessness and despair, to faith and courage. Spiritual guidance has a vertical upreach and a horizontal outreach. It is guided by the North Star of the heavens. Spiritual guidance is the path of truth and righteous that ultimately leads to a city called heaven whose builder and maker is God.

SPIRITUAL GUIDANCE

Lift up your heads, O ye gates; and be ye lift up, ye everlasting doors; and the king of glory shall come in.

    Psalm 24:7

That thou mayest walk in the way of good men, and keep the paths of righteousness.

    Proverbs 2:20

O house of Jacob, come ye, and let us walk in the light of the Lord.

    Isaiah 2:5

Arise, shine, thy light is come.

    Isaiah 60:1

SPIRITUAL GUIDANCE

Remember now thy creator in the days of thy youth.

   Ecclesiastes 12:1

Turn ye, Turn ye from your evil ways; For why will ye die, O house of Israel?

   Ezekiel 33:11

Ask for the old paths, where is the good way, and walk therein, and ye shall find rest for your souls.

   Jeremiah 6:16

Seek ye first the kingdom of God and his righteousness.

   Matthews 6:33

SPIRITUAL GUIDANCE

Ask and it shall be given you; Seek and ye shall find; knock and it shall be opened unto you.

    Luke 11:9

Jesus saith unto him, I am the way, the truth, and the life.

    John 14:6

Men ought always to pray, and not faint.

    Luke 18:1

Let us therefore follow after the things which make for peace.

    Romans 14:19

SPIRITUAL GUIDANCE

Let us cast off the works of darkness and let us put on the armour of light.

    Romans 13:12

Follow after charity and desire spiritual gifts.

    I Corinthians 14:1

Walk worthy of the vocation wherewith ye are called.

    Ephesians 4:1

Be ye therefore followers of God as dear children.

    Ephesians 5:1

SPIRITUAL GUIDANCE

Let the peace of God rule in your hearts.

   Colossians 3:15

Follow that which is good, both, among yourselves, and to all men.

   I Thessalonians 5:15

Follow righteousness, faith, charity, peace, with them that call on the Lord out of a pure heart.

   II Timothy 2:22

Follow peace with all men, and holiness, without which no man shall see the Lord.

   Hebrews 12:14

SPIRITUAL GUIDANCE

He that saith he abideth in him ought himself also so to walk, even as he walked.

   I John 2:6

Be not afraid, only believe.

   Mark 5:36

Chapter 9

Spiritual Appeal

The Bible is filled with spiritual appeals. It is filled with prayers and petitions that invoke the mercy of God. When natural disasters and the calamities of wars have plagued God's people they have petitioned God. When man's inhumanity to man has been unbearable, appeals have gone up to God. When the burdens of depression and guilt have been too overwhelming, man has cried out to God for relief.

Human crises and human needs often exceed the human capability of meeting those needs. When no human help can be found and when human help and human resources are inadequate for the crises and emergency at hand, spiritual appeal is the only viable option available.

Humanity is blessed with the Mighty God who is merciful and compassionate to listen to those who humble themselves and repent of their sins and cry out for help and mercy. It is comforting to know that there is an appeal beyond humanity. It is a reassuring blessing that there is a Righteous Judge who has jurisdiction over the courts and judicial systems of the world. This Judge sees all, knows all and looks on the heart.

SPIRITUAL APPEAL

Then Peter said unto them, repent, and be baptized every one of you in the name of Jesus Christ for the remission of sins and ye shall receive the gift of the Holy Ghost.

   Acts 2:38

Repent ye therefore, and be converted that your sins may be blotted out.

   Acts 3:19

And they stoned Stephen, calling upon God, and saying, Lord Jesus, receive my spirit. And he kneeled down, and cried with a loud voice, Lord, lay not this sin to their charge.

   Acts 7:59-60

Likewise the Spirit also helpeth our infirmities: for we know not what we should pray for as we ought: but the Spirit itself maketh intercession for us with groanings which cannot be uttered.

   Romans 8:26

SPIRITUAL APPEAL

And the Publican, standing afar off, would not lift up so much as his eyes unto heaven, but smote upon his breast, saying, God be merciful to me a sinner.

   Luke 18:13

And he said unto Jesus, Lord, remember me when thou comest into thy kingdom.

   Luke 23:42

Father, if thou be willing, remove this cup from me: nevertheless not my will, but thine, be done.

   Luke 22:42

Two blind men followed him, crying, Thou Son of David, have mercy on us.

   Matthew 9:27

SPIRITUAL APPEAL

Ask, and it shall be given you; seek, and ye shall find; knock, and it shall be opened unto you.

   Matthew 7:7

Simon, Simon, behold, Satan hath desired to have you, that he may sift you as wheat: But I have prayed for thee, that thy faith fail not.

   Luke 22:31, 32

And behold, a woman of Canaan came out of the same coasts, and cried unto him, saying, Have mercy on me, O Lord, thou Son of David; my daughter is greviously vexed with a devil.

   Matthew 15:22

O my Father, if this cup may not pass from me, except I drink it, Thy will be done.

   Matthew 26:42

SPIRITUAL APPEAL

Give therefore thy servant an understanding heart to judge thy people, that I may discern between good and bad.

   I Kings 3:9

Open thou mine eyes, that I may behold wondrous things out of thy law.

   Psalms 119:18

This poor man cried, and the Lord heard him, and saved him out of all his troubles.

   Psalms 34:6

Let the words of my mouth, and the meditation of my heart, be acceptable in thy sight, O Lord, my Strength and my Redeemer.

   Psalms 19:14

SPIRITUAL APPEAL

Give ear to my prayer, O God; and hide not thyself from my supplication.

Psalms 55:1

In my distress I cried unto the Lord, and he heard me. Deliver my soul, O Lord, from lying lips and from a deceitful tongue.

Psalms 120:1-2

Deliver me, O Lord, from the evil man: preserve me from the violent man.

Psalms 140:1

Deliver me from my persecutors; for they are stronger than I...Bring my soul out of prison, that I may praise thy name.

Psalms 142:6-7

God's Spiritual Prescriptions
For Healing, Liberation and Salvation

SPIRITUAL APPEAL

From the end of the earth will I cry unto thee, when my heart is overwhelmed: lead me to the rock that is higher than I.

Psalms 61:2

And when Esau heard the words of his father, he cried with a great and exceeding bitter cry, and said unto his father, Bless me, even me also, O my father.

Genesis 27:34

But think on me when it shall be well with thee, and shew kindness, I pray thee unto me, and make mention of me unto Pharaoh, and bring me out of this house.

Genesis 40:14

And Samuel cried unto the Lord for Israel; and the Lord heard him.

I Samuel 7:9

SPIRITUAL APPEAL

And Samson called unto the Lord, and said, O Lord God, remember me, I pray thee.

   Judges 16:28

The children of Israel sighed by reason of the bondage, and they cried, and their cry came up unto God by reason of their bondage.

   Exodus 2:23

Create in me a clean heart, O God; and renew a right spirit within me.

   Psalms 51:10

Cast me not away from thy presence, and take not thy Holy Spirit from me.

   Psalms 51:11

SPIRITUAL APPEAL

Evening, and morning, and at noon, will I pray, and cry aloud: and he shall hear my voice.

Psalms 55:17

Have mercy upon me, O Lord; for I am weak: O Lord, heal me: for my bones are vexed.

Psalms 6:2

If my people, which are called by my name, shall humble themselves, and pray, and seek my face, and turn from their wicked ways; then will I hear from heaven, and will forgive their sin, and will heal their land.

II Chronicles 7:14

Deliver me, I pray thee, from the hand of my brother, from the hand of Esau; for I fear him, lest he will come and smite me, and the mother with the children.

Genesis 32:11

Chapter 10

Spiritual Power

Spiritual power is from God and the Nature of God. The Gospel of John says that God is spirit and they that worship God must worship God in spirit and in truth. This God spiritual power is beyond human comprehension. The finite mind cannot comprehend the ageless, unlimited, all powerful, all knowing and everywhere present God. And yet God has revealed to the finite mind of man that the ultimate spiritual power of God is real.

The evidence of this mind boggling power of God is seen in the universe itself. The trillions, perhaps, zillions of celestial bodies are suspended in space. A power beyond the imagination of man brought the stars, solar systems and galaxies into existence and continue to sustain them in cosmos, not chaos. The sustaining power of the universe cannot be seen or heard by the natural senses of man. However, our natural senses tell us that the power is there.

In viewing the glory of God in the heavens, the Psalmist raised a most intriguing question, "What is man that Thou are mindful of him?" What is it about finite, powerless man that the omnipotent God would be concerned about him? The fact that God is concerned about mankind and that he made man in his image is good news. God has created a creature with a spiritual connection with God.

The Bible is a sacred historical record based on the operation of spiritual power. Through the working of the Holy Spirit the people of God have come out of darkness into his marvelous light. The Gospel of St. John Declares, "to them that believe, gave he power to become the sons of God." (John 1:12, RSV)

SPIRITUAL POWER

In the beginning God created the heaven and the earth... And God said, let there be light: and there was light.

   Genesis 1:1, 3

And Moses stretched out his hand over the sea; and the Lord caused the sea to go back by a strong east wind all that night, and made the sea dry land, and the waters were divided.

   Exodus 14:21

And the children of Israel went into the midst of the sea upon the dry ground.

   Exodus 14:22

And the Lord said unto Moses, stretch out thine hand over the sea, that the waters may come again upon the Egyptians, upon their chariots, and upon their horsemen.

   Exodus 14:26

SPIRITUAL POWER

And, behold, the veil of the temple was rent in twain from the top to the bottom, and the earth did quake, and the rocks rent; and the graves were opened, and many bodies of the saints which slept arose.

Matthew 27:51-52

And when the disciples saw him walking on the sea, they were troubled, saying it is a spirit; and they cried out for fear. But straightway Jesus spoke unto them, saying. Be of good cheer; It is I; be not afraid.

Matthew 14:26-27

The blind receive their sight, and the lame walk, the lepers are cleansed, and the deaf hear, the dead are raised up, and the poor have the Gospel preached to them.

Matthew 11:5

And Jesus went about all the cities and villages, teaching in their synagogues, and preaching the Gospel of the Kingdom, and healing every sickness and every disease among the people.

Matthew 9:35

SPIRITUAL POWER

He is not here: for he is risen, as he said. Come see, the place where the Lord lay. And go quickly, and tell his disciples that he is risen from the dead.

   Matthew 28:6-7

And Jesus came and spoke unto them, saying, All power is given unto me in heaven and in earth.

   Matthew 28:18

And he arose, and rebuked the wind, and said unto the sea, peace, be still and the wind ceased and there was a great calm.

   Mark 4:39

But as many as received him to them he gave power to become the sons of God, even to them that believe on his name.

   John 1:12

SPIRITUAL POWER

Jesus said unto her. I am the resurrection, and the life: he that believeth in me, though he were dead, yet shall he live.

John 11:25

And whosoever liveth and believeth in me shall never die.

John 11:26

And he that was dead came forth, bound hand and foot with grave clothes: and his face was bound about with a napkin. Jesus saith unto them. Loose him, and let him go.

John 11:44

He that believeth on me, the works that I do shall he do also: and greater works than these shall he do; because I go unto my Father.

John 14:12

SPIRITUAL POWER

And suddenly there came a sound from heaven as of a rushing mighty wind, and it filled all the house where they were sitting. And there appeared unto them cloven tongues like as of fire, and it sat upon each of them. And they were all filled with the Holy Ghost, and began to speak with other tongues, as the Spirit gave them utterance.

   Acts 2:2-4

While Peter yet spoke these words, the Holy Ghost fell on all them which heard the word.

   Acts 10:44

And, behold, the Angel of the Lord came upon him, and a light shined in the prison: And he smote Peter on the side, and raised him up, saying, arise up quickly. And his chains fell off from his hands.

   Acts 12:7

And at midnight Paul and Silas prayed, and sang praises unto God: and suddenly there was a great earthquake, so that the foundations of the prison were shaken: And immediately all the doors were opened, and everyone's bonds were loosed.

   Acts 16:25-26

SPIRITUAL POWER

By faith they passed through the Red Sea as by dry land; which the Egyptians assaying to do were drowned.

Hebrews 11:29

By faith the walls of Jericho fell down, after they were compassed about seven days.

Hebrews 11:30

Who through faith subdued kingdoms, wrought righteousness, obtained promises, stopped the mouths of lions.

Hebrews 11:33

(Who through faith) quenched the violence of fire, escaped the edge of the sword, out of weakness were made strong, waxed valiant in fight, turned to flight the armies of the aliens.

Hebrews 11:34

SPIRITUAL POWER

I am Alpha and Omega, the beginning and the ending, saith the Lord, which is, and which was, and which is to come, the Almighty.

   Revelation 1:8

I am Alpha and Omega, the first and the last.

   Revelation 1:11

Fear not, I am the first and the last; I am he that liveth, and was dead; and behold, I am alive forever more, Amen; and have the keys of hell and of death.

   Revelation 1:17-18

I am Alpha and Omega, the beginning and the end, the first and the last....I am the root and offspring of David, and the bright and morning star.

   Revelation 22:13, 16

Chapter 11

Spiritual Deliverance and Restoration

The Bible is the classic literature of all time that demonstrates God's power in delivering his human creatures from all manner of evil, diseases and disasters. As long as there is sin, famine, disease, the ill will of others, suffering and death, there is a need for deliverance and restoration. Ultimately, these urgent and vital needs exceed the power of humans to meet and satisfy. Only God can satisfy mankind's ultimate need for spiritual deliverance and restoration. A sober, objective and realistic assessment of the predicament of mankind must conclude, that we humans are totally and absolutely dependent upon God.

It is comforting and reassuring to have an unprecedented historical record that illustrates God's intervention in delivering and restoring his people. This record is the Bible. The Bible is not just past history. It is a promise of present help, future prophecy and the only real hope and real help for mankind's mortal human predicament. We human beings have fragile bodies, minds and spirits. Ultimately, without God, we will lose the battle against the evil and natural forces that seek our destruction.

In a world that is hazardous to our frailties and fragility and not always congenial to our human spirits, we have clear revelatory evidence that God promises deliverance to us. He has the compassion, mercy and the power to deliver us from sorrow to joy, from death to life, from time to eternity.

SPIRITUAL DELIVERANCE AND RESTORATION

Create in me a clean heart, O God; and renew a right spirit within me.

> *Psalm 51:10*

Restore unto me the Joy of thy salvation.

> *Psalm 51:12*

In God is my salvation and my glory.

> *Psalm 62:7*

Deliver me O God out of the hand of the wicked.

> *Psalm 71:4*

SPIRITUAL DELIVERANCE AND RESTORATION

He shall deliver the needy when he crieth: the poor also, and him that have no helper.

   Psalm 72:12

O let not the oppressed return ashamed: Let the poor and needy praise thy name.

   Psalm 74:21

Thus said the Lord God unto these bones; behold, I will cause breath to enter into you, and ye shall live.

   Ezekiel 37:5

He answered and said, Lo, I see four men loose, walking in the midst of the fire, and they have no hurt: and the form of the fourth is like the son of God.

   Daniel 3:25

SPIRITUAL DELIVERANCE AND RESTORATION

He delivereth and rescueth, and he worketh signs and wonders in heaven and in earth, who hath delivered Daniel from the power of the lions.

Daniel 6:27

My God hath sent his angel, and hath shut the lions' mouths that they have not hurt me.

Daniel 6:22

The blind receive their sight, the lame walk, the lepers cleansed, the deaf hear, the dead are raised up, and the poor have the Gospel preached to them.

Matthew 11:5

And they come to Jesus, and see him that was possessed with the devil, and had the legion; sitting, and clothed, and in his right mind.

Mark 5:15

SPIRITUAL DELIVERANCE AND RESTORATION

He hath sent me to heal the broken hearted, to preach deliverance to the captives, and recovering of sight to the blind, to set at liberty them that are bruised.

Luke 4:18

And when he thus had spoken, he cried with a loud voice, Lazarus, come forth. And he that was dead come forth.

John 11:43-44

Being justified by faith we have peace with God.

Romans 5:1

Humble yourselves therefore under the mighty hand of God, that he may exalt you in due time.

I Peter 5:6

Chapter 12

Spiritual Affirmation

Spiritual affirmation is divine reassurance against the oppressive negations in life. In a world that often rejects us, subordinates and slams doors in our faces, spiritual affirmation is the Believer's prescription for maintaining sanity and self worth. Affirmation is the opposite of negation. Negation destroys dignity and robs us of our humanity. Affirmation restores dignity and builds up humanity. Negations send messages that "you are nobody," "you don't count," "you cannot do anything that merits positive recognition." Spiritual affirmation refutes these negative claims.

Spiritual affirmation is reassurance from above. It rekindles hope and faith and sometimes joy, even in the midst of heartbreaking sorrows. Spiritual affirmation helps us to reflect on the promises of God and God's inexhaustible resources of help and hope. Spiritual affirmation from scripture provides the message that we are the children of God who will never be forsaken by God.

Spiritual affirmation not only helps cope with the adversities of life, but also helps us to live victoriously and triumphantly with the knowledge of God's unconditional love. There is a recurring theme throughout the Scriptures from Genesis through Revelation that mankind is significantly important to God. God's concern for mankind is expressed by the prophets, through the Law and in Jesus Christ.

SPIRITUAL AFFIRMATION

All the days of my appointed time will I wait till my change come.

   Job 14:14

And they shall know that I am the Lord.

   Ezekiel 12:15

He taught them as one having authority.

   Matthew 7:29

O woman great is thy faith.

   Matthew 15:28

SPIRITUAL AFFIRMATION

Upon this rock I will build my church, and the gates of hell shall not prevail against it.

Matthew 16:18

The crooked shall be made straight.

Luke 3:5

My grace is sufficient for thee.

II Corinthians 12:9

I can do all things through Christ which strengthens me.

Philippians 4:13

SPIRITUAL AFFIRMATION

At the name of Jesus every knee should bow, and every tongue should confess, that Jesus Christ is Lord.

Philippians 2:10-11

There is neither Jew nor Greek, there is neither bond nor free, there is neither male nor female: For ye are all one in Christ Jesus.

Galatians 3:28

I press toward the mark for the prize of the high calling of God in Christ Jesus.

Philippians 3:14

I have fought a good fight. I have finished my course. I have kept the faith.

II Timothy 4:7

Chapter 13

Spiritual Rewards

The Believer must know that his/her faith in God and service to humanity are not in vain. There is an inherent and undeniable law of compensation. This law mandates that you reap what you sow. Somehow, a person gets out of life what he or she puts into life.

There is even a law of physics that substantiates, that for every action, there is an equal and opposite reaction. The Bible declares that heavenly rewards are more definite and more secure than earthly rewards. Treasures laid up in heaven do not corrupt or get stolen by thieves.

Since there are no guaranties in our earthly living, the investment in spiritual rewards must be the top priority. Living the righteous life by faith not only accumulates rewards in heaven, but it optimizes the spiritual rewards in this life. Love for God compels a stronger love for mankind. The knowledge by faith that your name is written in heaven provides a present and perpetual joy. The spiritual rewards and benefits of heaven are enjoyed as we journey through this life on our way to that wonderful and glorious eternal destination.

It is sin, unrighteous and injustice that robs us of our spiritual rewards. A life dedicated to overcoming these failures and curses for ourselves and others put stars in our crown and peace in our hearts. There is a reward in fighting the good fight of faith. There may not be material rewards at the end of our journey. However, a clear conscience is a priceless reward.

Those who believe in Christ find joy in serving, sharing, giving, living and even dying. Spiritual rewards begin now and last forever.

SPIRITUAL REWARDS

If my people, which are called by my name, shall humble themselves, and pray, and seek my face, and turn from their wicked ways, then will I hear from heaven, and will forgive their sin, and will heal their land.

   II Chronicles 7:14

The gift of God is eternal life through Jesus Christ.

   Romans 6:23

The Kindgom of God is not meat and drink; but righteousness, and peace, and Joy in the Holy Ghost.

   Romans 14:17

Eye hath not seen, nor ear heard, neither have entered into the heart of man, the things which God hath prepared for them that love him.

   I Corinthians 2:9

SPIRITUAL REWARDS

And ye shall be hated of all men for my name's sake: but he that endureth to the end shall be saved.

   Matthew 10:22

Take my yoke upon you, and learn of me: for I am meek and lowly in heart: and ye shall find rest unto your souls.

   Matthew 11:29

For thou shalt be recompensed at the resurrection of the just.

   Luke 14:14

Rejoice because your names are written in heaven.

   Luke 10:20

SPIRITUAL REWARDS

For God so loved the world, that he gave his only begotten Son, that whosoever believeth in him should not perish, but have eternal life.

   John 3:16

Lo, I am with you alway, even unto the end of the world.

   Matthew 28:20

I am the bread of life: he that cometh to me shall never hunger; and he that believeth on me shall never thirst.

   John 6:35

I am the resurrection, and the life: he that believeth in me, though he were dead, yet shall he live: and whosover liveth and believeth in me shall never die.

   John 11:25-26

SPIRITUAL REWARDS

Let not your heart be troubled: neither let it be afraid.

   John 14:27

Peace I leave with you. My peace I give unto you: not as the world giveth, give I unto you.

   John 14:27

Because I live, ye shall live also.

   John 14:19

Fear not little flock, for it is your Father's good pleasure to give you the kingdom.

   Luke 12:32

SPIRITUAL REWARDS

And the peace of God, which passeth all understanding, shall keep your hearts and minds through Christ Jesus.

   Philippians 4:7

Hence forth there is laid up for me a crown of righteousness, which the Lord, the righteous judge, shall give me at that day: and not to me only, but unto all them also that love his appearing.

   II Timothy 4:8

Blessed is the man that endureth temptation: for when he is tried, he shall receive the crown of life, which the Lord hath promised to them that love him.

   James 1:12

Nevertheless we, according to his promise, look for new heavens and a new earth, wherein dwelleth righteousness.

   II Peter 3:13

SPIRITUAL REWARDS

Ye shall receive a crown of glory that fade not a way.

   I Peter 5:4

Be thou faithful unto death, and I will give thee a crown of life.

   Revelation 2:10

And he that overcometh, and keepeth my works unto the end, to him will I give power over the nations.

   Revelation 2:26

To him that overcometh will I grant to sit with me in my throne.

   Revelation 3:21

SPIRITUAL REWARDS

For the lamb which is in the midst of the throne shall feed them, and shall lead them unto living fountains of waters: and God shall wipe away all tears from their eyes.

Revelation 7:17

He that overcometh shall inherit all things; and I will be his God and he shall be my son.

Revelation 21:7

For we know that if our earthy house of this tabernacle were dissolved, we have a building of God, an house not made with hands, eternal in the heavens.

II Corinthians 5:1

As we have borne the image of the earthy, we shall also bear the image of the heavenly.

I Corinthians 15:49

Chapter 14

Spiritual Salvation

If the soul *is* lost everything is lost, because the scripture teaches that "flesh and blood" cannot inherit the Kingdom of God. It teaches further that all have sinned and come short of the glory of God and that the soul that sins shall die. All persons everywhere stand in need of spiritual salvation. No person has the power to save him or herself. Without God's mercy and grace all persons are helplessly and hopelessly lost.

It is God's will to save man from the destruction of sin and death. The whole Bible is good news from God because it contains God's plan for the spiritual salvation of mankind. Since God created man with a free will man must choose between good and evil, life and death. The Bible is replete with the stories of men, women, groups and nations making choices between good and evil and reaping the consequences.

God's will and his desire to save man is so strong that he sent priests, judges, kings, lawgivers and prophets with salvation messages. But the disobedience of man was so profound that God gave his only begotten Son to save the world. The simple requirement for spiritual salvation is to receive the gift, Jesus Christ, as Lord and Savior.

Spiritual salvation is not exclusive of personal, social, economic and political salvation. God is interested in the total life of mankind. This includes body, mind and soul, here, and in the hereafter. The new spiritual life in Jesus Christ is the reborn more abundant life.

SPIRITUAL SALVATION

But lay up for yourselves treasures in heaven, where neither moth nor rust doth corrupt, and where thieves do not break through nor steal.

Matthew 6:20

But seek ye first the Kingdom of God, and his righteousness: and all these things shall be added unto you.

Matthew 6:33

And he said unto them, Go ye into all the world, and preach the gospel to every creature. He that believeth and is baptized shall be saved; but he that believeth not shall be damned.

Mark 16:15-16

Now when Jesus heard these things, he said unto him, yet lackest thou one thing: sell all that thou hast, and distribute unto the poor, and thou shalt have treasure in heaven: and come, follow me.

Luke 18:22

SPIRITUAL SALVATION

And he said unto Jesus, Lord, remember me when thou comest into thy kingdom. And Jesus said unto him verily I say unto thee, today shalt thou be with me in paradise.

   Luke 23:42-43

But as many as received him, to them gave he power to become the sons of God, even to them that believe on his name.

   John 1:12

Jesus answered and said unto him, verily, verily, I say unto thee, except a man be born again, he cannot see the Kingdom of God... Marvel not that I said unto thee, ye must be born again.

   John 3:3, 7

He that believeth on the Son hath everlasting life: and he that believeth not the Son shall not see life.

   John 3:36

SPIRITUAL SALVATION

For I am not ashamed of the Gospel of Christ: for it is the power of God unto salvation to everyone that believeth.

Romans 1:16

Therefore, being justified by faith, we have peace with God through our Lord Jesus Christ.

Romans 5:1

For he that is dead is freed from sin. Now if we be dead with Christ, we believe that we shall also live with him.

Romans 6:7-8

For the wages of sin is death; but the gift of God is eternal life through Jesus Christ our Lord.

Romans 6:23

SPIRITUAL SALVATION

Neither is there salvation in any other: for there is none other name under heaven given among men, whereby we must be saved.

   Acts 4:12

And by him all that believe are justified from all things, from which ye could not be justified by the law of Moses.

   Acts 13:39

But we believe that through the grace of the Lord Jesus Christ we shall be saved.

   Acts 15:11

And they said, Believe on the Lord Jesus Christ, and thou shalt be saved, and thy house.

   Acts 16:31

SPIRITUAL SALVATION

Labour not for the meat which perisheth, but for that meat which endureth unto everlasting life, which the Son of man shall give unto you: for him hath the Father sealed.

   John 6:27

Verily, verily, I say unto you, he that believeth on me hath everlasting life.

   John 6:47

I said therefore unto you, that ye shall die in your sins: for if ye believe not that I am He, ye shall die in your sins.

   John 8:24

Jesus said unto her, I am the resurrection and the life: he that believeth in me, though he were dead, yet shall he live.

   John 11:25

SPIRITUAL SALVATION

Therefore I endure all things for the elect's sakes, that they may also obtain the salvation which is in Christ Jesus with eternal glory.

II Timothy 2:10

And that from a child thou hast known the holy Scriptures, which are able to make thee wise unto salvation through faith which is in Christ Jesus.

II Timothy 3:15

How shall we escape, if we neglect so great salvation.

Hebrews 2:3

And being made perfect, he became the author of eternal salvation unto all them that obey him.

Hebrews 5:9

Chapter 15

Frames and Prescriptions
of
Inspiration and Truth

TRUST IN THE LIVING GOD NOT UNCERTAIN RICHES

Charge them that are rich in this world, that they be not highminded, nor trust in uncertain riches, but in the living God, who giveth us richly all things to enjoy;

That they do good, that they be rich in good works, ready to distribute, willing to communicate;

Laying up in store for themselves a good foundation against the time to come, that they may lay hold on eternal life.

I Timothy 6:17-19

BE NOT CONFORMED TO THIS WORLD

I beseech you therefore, brethren, by the mercies of God, that ye present your bodies a living sacrifice, holy, acceptable unto God, which is your reasonable service.

And be not conformed to this world: but be ye transformed by the renewing of your mind, that ye may prove what is that good, and acceptable, and perfect, will of God.

Romans 12:1-2

FLEE TEMPTATIONS-FOLLOW RIGHTEOUSNESS

But they that will be rich fall into temptation and a snare, and into many foolish and hurtful lusts, which drown men in destruction and perdition.

For the love of money is the root of all evil: which while some coveted after, they have erred from the faith, and pierced themselves through with many sorrows.

But thou, O man of God, flee these things; and follow after righteousness, godliness, faith, love, patience, meekness.

Fight the good fight of faith, lay hold on eternal life, whereunto thou art also called, and hast professed a good profession before many witnesses.

I Timothy 6:9-12

THROUGH FAITH

Who though faith subdued kingdoms, wrought righteousness, obtained promises, stopped the mouths of lions,

Quenched the violence of fire, escaped the edge of the sword, out of weakness were made strong, waxed valiant in fight, turned to flight the armies of the aliens.

Women received their dead raised to life again: and others were tortured, not accepting deliverance; that they might obtain a better resurrection.

Hebrews 11:33-35

CHOSEN TO BE A SOLDIER

Thou therefore, my son, be strong in the grace that is in Christ Jesus.

And the things that thou hast heard of me among many witnesses, the same commit thou to faithful men, who shall be able to teach others also.

Thou therefore endure hardness, as a good soldier of Jesus Christ.

No man that warreth entangleth himself with the affairs of this life; that he may please him who hath chosen him to be a soldier.

II Timothy 2:1-4

FAMILY INSTRUCTIONS

Let the word of Christ dwell in you richly in all wisdom; teaching and admonishing one another in psalms and hymns and spiritual songs, singing with grace in your hearts to the Lord.

And whatsoever ye do in word or deed, do all in the name of the Lord Jesus, giving thanks to God and the Father by him.

Wives, submit yourselves unto your own husbands, as it is fit in the Lord.

Husbands, love your wives, and be not bitter against them.

Children, obey your parents in all things: for this is well pleasing unto the Lord.

Fathers, provoke not your children to anger, lest they be discouraged.

Colossians 3:16-21

RESPECT FAMILY MEMBERS

Rebuke not an elder, but intreat him as a father, and the younger men as brethren;

The elder women as mothers; the younger as sisters, with all purity.

Honor widows that are widows indeed.

But if any widows have children or nephews, let them learn first to shew piety at home, and to requite their parents: for that is good and acceptable before God.

I Timothy 5:1-4

IF THE WORLD HATE YOU

If the world hate you, ye know that it hated me before it hated you.

If ye were of the world, the world would love his own: but because ye are not of the world, but I have chosen you out of the world, therefore the world hateth you.

Remember the word that I said unto you, The servant is not greater than his Lord. If they have persecuted me, they will also persecute you: if they have kept my saying, they will keep yours also.

But all these things will they do unto you for my name's sake, because they know not him that sent me.

If I had not come and spoken unto them, they had not had sin: but now they have no cloke for their sin.

He that hateth me hateth my father also.

John 15:18-23

OUR HIGH PRIEST IN JESUS

For the Word of God is quick, and powerful, and sharper than any two-edged sword, piercing even to the dividing asunder of soul and spirit, and of the joints and marrow, and is a discerner of the thoughts and intents of the heart.

Neither is there any creature that is not manifest in his sight: but all things are naked and opened unto the eyes of him with whom we have to do.

Seeing then that we have a great high priest, that is passed into the heavens, Jesus the Son of God, let us hold fast our profession.

For we have not an high priest which cannot be touched with the feeling of our infirmities; but was in all points tempted like as we are, yet without sin.

Let us therefore come boldly unto the throne of grace, that we may obtain mercy, and find grace to help in time of need.

Hebrews 4:12-16

WARNING OF THE WATCHMAN

But if the watchman see the sword come, and blow not the trumpet, and the people be not warned; if the sword come, and take any person from among them, he is taken away in his iniquity; but his blood will I require at the watchman's hand.

So thou, O son of man, I have set thee a watchman unto the house of Israel; therefore thou shalt hear the word at my mouth, and warn them from me.

When I say unto the wicked, O wicked man, thou shalt surely die; if thou dost not speak to warn the wicked from his way, that wicked man shall die in his iniquity; but his blood will I require at thine hand.

Nevertheless, if thou warn the wicked of his way to turn from it; if he do not turn from his way, he shall die in his iniquity; but thou hast delivered thy soul.

Therefore, O thou son of man, speak unto the house of Israel: thus ye speak, saying, If our transgressions and our sins be upon us, and we pine away in them, how should we then live?

Say unto them as I live, saith the Lord God, I have no pleasure in the death of the wicked; but that the wicked turn from his way and live; turn ye, turn ye from your evil ways; for why will ye die, O house of Israel?

Ezekiel 33:6-11

THE PRODIGAL SON

And he said, A certain man had two sons:

And the younger of them said to his father, Father, give me the portion of goods that falleth to me. And he divided unto them his living.

And not many days after the younger son gathered all together, and took his journey into a far country, and there wasted his substance with riotous living.
Luke 15:11-13

And when he came to himself, he said, How many hired servants of my father's have bread enough and to spare, and I perish with hunger!

I will arise and go to my father, and will say unto him, Father, I have sinned against heaven, and before thee,

And am no more worthy to be called thy son: make me as one of thy hired servant.

And he arose, and came to his father. But when he was yet a great way off, his father saw him, and had compassion, and ran, and fell on his neck, and kissed him.

And the son said unto him, Father, I have sinned against heaven, and in thy sight, and am no more worthy to be called thy son.

But the father said to his servants, Bring forth, the best robe, and put it on him; and put a ring on his hand, and shoes on his feet:

And bring hither the fatted calf, and kill it; and let us eat, and be merry:

For this my son was dead, and is alive again; he was lost, and is found. And they began to be merry.
Luke 15:17-24

THE SPIRIT OF THE LORD IS UPON ME

And he came to Nazareth, where he had been brought up: and, as his custom was, he went into the synagogue on the Sabbath Day, and stood up for to read.

And there was delivered unto him the book of the prophet Isaiah. And when he had open the book, he found the place where it was written,

The Spirit of the Lord is upon me, because he hath anointed me to preach the gospel to the poor; he hath sent me to heal the brokenhearted, to preach deliverance to the captives, and recovering of sight to the blind, to set at liberty them that are bruised,

To preach the acceptable year of the Lord.

And he closed the book, and he gave it again to the minister, and sat down. And the eyes of all them that were in the synagogue were fastened on him.

And he began to say unto them, This day is this scripture fulfilled in your ears.

Luke 4:16-21

THE PRAYER OF A PHARISEE AND PUBLICAN

Two men went up into the temple to pray; the one a Pharisee, and the other a publican.

The Pharisee stood and prayed thus with himself, God, I thank thee, that I am not as other men are, extortioners, unjust, adulterers, or even as this publican.

I fast twice in the week, I give tithes of all that I possess.

And the publican, standing afar off, would not lift up so much as his eyes unto heaven, but smote upon his breast, saying, God, be merciful to me a sinner.

I tell you, this man went down to his house justified rather than the other: for every one that exalteth himself shall be abased; and he that humbleth himself shall be exalted.

Luke 18:10-14

TEN MEN HEALED OF LEPROSY

And it came to pass, as he went to Jerusalem, that he passed through the midst of Samaria and Galilee.

And as he entered into a certain village, there met him ten men that were lepers, which stood afar off:

And they lifted up their voices, and said, Jesus, Master, have mercy on us.

And when he saw them, he said unto them, Go shew yourselves unto the priests, And it came to pass, that, as they went, they were cleansed.

And one of them, when he saw that he was healed, turned back, and with a loud voice glorified God.

And fell down on his face at his feet, giving him thanks: and he was a Samaritan.

And Jesus answering said, were there not ten cleansed? But where are the nine?

There are not found that returned to give glory to God, save this stranger.

And he said unto him, Arise, go thy way: Thy faith hath made thee whole.

Luke 17:11-19

HE IS NOT HERE, BUT IS RISEN

Now upon the first day of the week. very early in the morning, they came unto the sepulchre, bringing the spices which they had prepared, and certain others with them.

And they found the stone rolled away from the sepulchre.

And they entered in, and found not the body of the Lord Jesus.

And it came to pass, as they were much perplexed thereabout, behold, two men stood by them in shining garments:

And as they were afraid, and bowed down their faces to the earth, they said unto them, Why seek ye the living among the dead?

He is not here, but is risen: remember how he spake unto you when was yet in Galilee,

Saying, the Son of Man must be delivered into the hands of sinful men, and be crucified, and the third day rise again.

And they remembered his words, And returned from the sepulchre, and told all these things unto the eleven, and to all the rest.

It was Mary Magdalene and Joanna, and Mary the mother of James, and other women that were with them, which told these things unto the apostles.

Luke 24:1-10

O JERUSALEM

By the rivers of Babylon, there we sat down, yea, we wept, when we remembered Zion.

We hanged our harps upon the willows in the midst thereof.

For there they that carried us away captive required of us a song; and they that wasted us required of us mirth, saying, Sing us one of the songs of Zion.

How shall we sing the Lord's song in a strange land?

If I forget thee, O Jerusalem, let my right hand forget her cunning.

If I do not remember thee, let my tongue cleave to the roof of my mouth; if I prefer not Jerusalem above my chief joy.

Psalm 137:1-6

FEED MY SHEEP

So when they had dined, Jesus saith to Simon Peter, Simon, son of Jonas, lovest thou me more than these? He saith unto him, yea, Lord: thou knowest that I love thee. He saith unto him, "Feed my lambs".

He saith to him again the second time, "Simon, son of Jonas, Lovest thou me?" He saith unto him, "Yea, Lord; thou knowest that I love thee. He saith unto him, "Feed my sheep".

He saith unto him the third time, "Simon, son of Jonas, lovest thou me?" Peter was grieved because he said unto him the third time, "Lovest thou me?" And he said unto him, "Lord, thou knowest all things: thou knowest that I love thee". Jesus saith unto him, "Feed my sheep".

John 21:15-17

A NEW COMMANDMENT

"Little children, yet a little while I am with you. You shall seek me: and as I said Unto the Jews, whither I go, ye cannot come; so now I say to you."

"A new commandment I give unto you, That ye love one another: as I have loved you, that ye also love one another."

"By this shall all men know that ye are my disciples, if ye have love one to another."

Simon Peter said unto him, Lord, whither goest thou? Jesus answered him, "Whither I go, thou canst not follow me now; but thou shalt follow me afterwards".

Peter said unto him, "Lord, why cannot I follow thee now? I will lay down my life for thy sake."

Jesus answered him, "Wilt thou lay down thy life for my sake? Verily, Verily, I say unto thee, the cock shall not crow, till thou hast denied me thrice".

John 13:33-38

God's Spiritual Prescriptions
For Healing, Liberation and Salvation

UPON THIS ROCK

When Jesus came into the coasts of Caesarea Philippi, he asked his disciples, saying, Who do men say that I the Son of man am?

And they said, Some say that thou art John the Baptist: some, Elias, and others, Jeremias, or one of the prophets.

He said unto them, but whom say ye that I am?

And Simon Peter answered and said, Thou art the Christ, the Son of the Living God.

And Jesus answered and said unto him, Blessed art thou, Simon Barjona: for flesh and blood hath not revealed it unto thee, but my Father which is in heaven.

And I say also unto thee, That thou art Peter, and upon this rock I will build my church; and the gates of hell shall not prevail against it.

Matthews 16:13-18

HARVEST GREAT, LABOURERS FEW

And Jesus went about all the cities and villages, teaching in their synagogues, and preaching the gospel of the kingdom, and healing every sickness and every disease among the people.

But when he saw the multitudes, he was moved with compassion on them, because they fainted, and were scattered abroad, as sheep having no shepherd.

Then saith he unto his disciples, The harvest truly is plenteous, but the labourers are few:

Pray ye therefore the Lord of the harvest, that he will send forth labourers into his harvest.

Matthews 9:35-38

THE RICH RULER

And a certain ruler asked him, saying, Good Master, what shall I do to inherit eternal life?

And Jesus said unto him, why callest thou me good? None is good, save one, that is, God.

Thou kowest the commandments, Do not commit adultery, Do not kill, Do not steal, Do not bear false witness, Honour thy father and thy mother.

And he said, All these have I kept from my youth up.

Now when Jesus heard these things, he said unto him, yet lackest thou one thing: sell all that thou hast, and distribute unto the poor, and thou shalt have treasure in heaven: and come follow me.

And when he heard this, he was very sorrowful: for he was very rich.

And when Jesus saw that he was very sorrowful, he said, How hardly shall they that have riches enter into the kingdom of God!

Luke 18:18-24

ZACCHAEUS SOUGHT TO SEE JESUS

And Jesus entered and passed through Jericho.

And behold, there was a man named Zacchaeus, which was the chief among the publicans, and he was rich.

And he sought to see Jesus who he was: and could not for the press, because he was little of stature.

And he ran before, and climbed up into a sycamore tree to see him: for he was to pass that way.

And when Jesus came to the place, he looked up, and saw him, and said unto him, Zacchaeus, make haste, and come down; for today I must abide at thy house.

And he made haste and came down, and received him joyfully.

And when they saw it, they all murmured, saying, That he was gone to be guest with a man that is a sinner.

And Zacchaeus stood, and said unto the Lord; Behold, Lord, the half of my goods I give to the poor; and if I have taken anything from any man by false accusation, I restore him fourfold.

And Jesus said unto him, This day is salvation come to this house, forsomuch as he also is a son of Abraham.

Luke 19:1-9

SEED THAT FALLS ON GOOD GROUND

A sower went out to sow his seed: and as he sowed, some fell by the way side-. And some fell upon a rock--and some fell among thorns-and others fell on good ground, and sprang up, and bare fruit an hundredfold. And when he had said these things, he cried, He that hath ears to hear, let him hear.

Luke 8:5-8

Now the parable is this: The seed is the word of God.

Those by the way side are they that hear; then cometh the devil, and taketh away the word out of their hearts, lest they should believe and be saved.

They on the rock are they, which, when they hear, receive the word with joy; and these have no root, which for a while believe, and in time of temptation fall away.

And that which fell among thorns are they, which, when they have heard, go forth, and are choked with cares and riches and pleasures of this life, and bring no fruit to perfection.

But that on the good ground are they, which in an honest and good heart, having heard the word, keep it, and bring forth fruit with patience.

Luke 8:11-15

Jesus Heals Canaanite's Daughter

And behold, a woman of Canaan came out of the same coasts, and cried unto him, saying, Have mercy on me, O Lord, thou Son of David; my daughter is grievously vexed with a devil.

But he answered her not a word, And his disciples came and besought him, saying, Send her away; for she crieth after us.

But he answered and said, I am not sent but unto the lost sheep of the house of Israel.

Then came she and worshipped him, saying, Lord, help me.

But he answered and said, It is not meet to take the children's bread, and to cast it to dogs.

And she said, Truth, Lord: yet the dogs eat of the crumbs which fall from their masters table.

Then Jesus answered and said unto her, O woman, great is thy faith: be It unto thee even as thou wilt. And her daughter was made whole from that very hour.

Matthew 15:22-28

GOD ANSWERS PRAYERS

And I say unto you, Ask, and it shall be given you; seek, and ye shall find; knock, and it shall be opened unto you.

For every one that asketh receiveth; and he that seeketh findeth; and to him that knocketh it shall be opened.

If a son shall ask bread of any of you that is a father, will he give him a stone? Or if he ask a fish, will he for a fish give him a serpent?

Or if he shall ask an egg, will he offer him a scorpion?

If ye then, being evil, know how to give good gifts unto your children: how much more shall your heavenly Father give the Holy Spirit to them that ask him?

Luke 11:9-13

PREPARE YE THE WAY OF THE LORD

Comfort ye, comfort ye my people, saith your God.

Speak ye comfortably to Jerusalem, and cry unto her, that her warfare is accomplished, that her iniquity is pardoned: for she hath received of the Lord's hand double for all her sins.

The voice of him that crieth in the wilderness. Prepare ye the way of the Lord, make straight in the desert a highway for our God.

Every valley shall be exalted, and every mountain and hill shall be made low: and the crooked shall be made straight, and the rough places plain:

And the glory of the Lord shall be revealed, and all flesh shall see it together: for the mouth of the Lord hath spoken it.

Isaiah 40:1-5

LET JUDGMENT RUN DOWN AS WATER

I hate, I despise your feast days, and I will not smell in your solemn assemblies.

Though ye offer me burnt offerings and your meat offerings, I will not accept them: neither will I regard the peace offerings of your fat beasts,

Take thou away from me the noise of thy songs; for I will not hear the melody of thy viols.

But let judgement run down as waters, and righteousness as a mighty stream.

Amos 5:21-24

WATCH, BE READY

Blessed are those servants, whom the Lord when he cometh shall find watching: verily I say unto you, that he shall gird himself, and make them to sit down to meat, and will come forth and serve them.

And if he shall come in the second watch, or come in the third watch, and find them so, blessed are those servants.

And this know, that if the good man of the house had known what hour the thief would come, he would have watched, and not have suffered his house to be broken through.

Be ye therefore ready also: for the Son of man cometh at an hour when ye think not.

Luke 12:37-40

A BLIND MAN RECEIVES SIGHT

And It came to pass, that as he was come nigh unto Jericho, a certain blind man sat by the way side begging:

And hearing the multitude pass by, he asked what it meant.

And they told him, that Jesus of Nazareth passeth by.

And he cried, saying, Jesus, thou son of David, have mercy on me.

And they which went before rebuked him, that he should hold his peace: but he cried so much the more, thou son of David, have mercy on me.

And Jesus stood, and commanded him to be brought unto him: and when he was come near, he asked him, saying, what wilt thou that I shall do unto thee? And he said, Lord, that I may receive my sight

And Jesus said unto him, Receive thy sight: thy faith had saved thee.

And immediately he received his sight, and followed him, glorifying God: and all the people, when they saw it, gave praise unto God.

Luke 18:35-43

MAN WHO BUILT A BIGGER BARN

And he spake a parable unto them, saying, The ground of a certain richman brought forth plentifully;

And he thought within himself, saying, what shall I do, because I have no room where to bestow my fruits?

And he said, this will I do: I will pull down my barns, and build greater; and there will I bestow all my fruits and my goods.

And I will say to my soul, soul, thou hast much goods laid up for many years; take thine ease, eat, drink, and be merry.

But God said unto him, thou fool, this night thy soul shall be required of thee: then whose shall those things be, which thou hast provided?

So is he that layeth up treasure for himself, and is not rich toward God.

Luke 12:16-21

SEEK THE KINGDOM FIRST

If then God so clothe the grass, which is to-day in the field, and to-morrow is cast into the oven; how much more will he clothe you, O ye of little faith?

And seek not ye what ye shall eat or what ye shall drink, neither be ye of doubtful mind.

For all these things do the nations of the world seek after: and your Father knoweth that ye have need of these things.

But rather seek ye the kingdom of God: and all these things shall be added unto you.

Fear not little flock; for it is our Father's good pleasure to give you the kingdom.

Luke 12:28-32

THE WIND AND THE WATER OBEY HIM

Now it came to pass on a certain day that he went into a ship with his disciples: and he said unto them, Let us go over unto the other side of the lake. And they launched forth.

But as they sailed he fell asleep: and there came down a storm of wind on the lake; and they were filled with water, and were in jeopardy.

And they came to him, and awoke him, saying, Master, Master, we perish. Then he arose, and rebuked the wind and the raging of the water: and they ceased, and there was a calm.

And he said unto them, where is your faith? And they being afraid wondered, saying one to another, what manner of man is this for he commandeth even the winds and water, and they obey him.

Luke 8:22-25

GO TELL JOHN

And John calling unto him two of his disciples sent them to Jesus, saying, art thou he that should come? Or look we for another?

When the men were come unto him, they said, John Baptist hath sent us unto thee, saying, Art thou he that should come? Or look we for another?

And in that same hour he cured many of their infirmities and plagues, and of evil spirits; and unto many that were blind he gave sight.

Then Jesus answering said unto them, Go your way, and tell John what things ye have seen and heard; how that the blind see, the lame walk, the lepers are cleansed, the deaf hear, the dead are raised, to the poor the gospel is preached.

And blessed is he, whosoever shall not be offended in me.

Luke 7:19-23

Willie James Webb

THE GREAT SUPPER INVITATIONS

Then said he unto him, A certain man made a great supper, and bade many:

And sent his servant at supper time to say to them that were bidden, Come; for all things are now ready.

And they all with one consent began to make excuse. The first said unto him, I have bought a piece of ground, and I must needs go and see it: I pray thee have me excused.

And another said, I have bought five yoke of oxen, and I go to prove them: I pray the have me excused.

And another, said I have married a wife, and therefore I cannot come.

So that servant came, and showed his Lord these things. Then the master of the house being angry said to his servant, Go out quickly into the streets and lanes of the city, and bring in hither the poor, and the maimed, and the halt, and the blind.

And the servant said, Lord, it is done as thou has commanded, and yet there is room.

And the Lord said unto the servant, Go out into the highways and hedges, and compel them to come in, that my house may be filled.

For I say unto you, that none of those men which were bidden shall taste of my supper.

Luke 14:16-24

HEALING FOR THE BLIND

And, behold, two blind men sitting by the way side, When they heard that Jesus passed by, cried out, saying, Have mercy on us, O Lord, thou Son of David.

And the multitude rebuked them, because they should hold their peace: but they cried the more, saying, Have mercy on us, O Lord, thou son of David.

And Jesus stood still, and called them, and said, What will ye that I shall do unto you?

They say unto Him, Lord, that our eyes may be opened.

So Jesus had compassion on them, and touched their eyes: and immediately their eyes received sight, and they followed him.

Matthews 20:30-34

WASHED – SANCTIFIED - JUSTIFIED

Know ye not that the unrighteous shall not inherit the kingdom of God? Be not deceived: neither fornicators, nor idolaters, nor adulterers, nor abusers of themselves with mankind,

Nor thieves, nor covetous, nor drunkards nor revilers, nor extortioners, shall inherit the kingdom of God.

And such were some of you: but ye are washed, but ye are sanctified, but ye are justified in the name of the Lord Jesus, and by the Spirit of our God.

All things are lawful unto me, but all things are not expedient: all things are lawful for me, but I will not be brought under the power of any.

I Corinthians 6:9-12

The Plea of Samson

And Samson called unto the Lord, and said, O Lord God, remember me, I pray thee, and strengthen me, I pray thee, only this once, O God, that I may be at once avenged of the philistines for my two eyes.

Judges 16:28

WHO IS GREAT?

And there was also a strife among them, which of them should be accounted the greatest.

And he said unto them, The Kings of the Gentiles exercise lordship over them; and they that exercise authority upon them are called benefactors.

But ye shall not be so: but he that is greatest among you, let him be as the younger; and he that is chief, as he that doth serve.

For whether is greater, he that sitteth at meat, or he that serveth? Is not he that sitteth at meat? but I am among you as he that serveth.

St. Luke 22:24-27

JESUS WASHED DISCIPLES' FEET

He riseth from supper and laid aside his garments: and took a towel, and girded himself.

After that he poureth water into a basin, and began to wash the disciples' feet, and to wipe them with the towel wherewith he was girded.

John 13:4-5

So after he had washed their feet, and had taken his garments, and was set down again, he said unto them, know ye what I have done to you?

Ye call me Master and Lord: and ye say well: for so am I.

If I then, your Lord and Master, have washed your feet; ye also ought to wash one another's feet.

John 13:12-14

Willie James Webb

RECONCILIATION

And there stood no man with him, while Joseph made himself known unto his brethren.

And he wept aloud: and the Egyptians and the house of Pharaoh heard.

And Joseph said unto his brethren, I am Joseph: doth my father yet live? And his brethren could not answer him; for they were troubled at his presence.

And Joseph said unto his brethren, Come near to me, I pray you. And they came near. And he said, I am Joseph your brother, whom ye sold into Egypt.

Now therefore be not grieved, nor angry with yourselves, that ye sold me hither: for God did send me before you to preserve life.

And God sent me before you to preserve you a posterity in the earth, and to save your lives by a great deliverance.

So now it was not you that sent me hither, but God: and he hath made me a father to Pharaoh, and lord of all his house, and a ruler throughout all the land of Egypt.

And thou shalt dwell in the land of Goshen, and thou shalt be near unto me, thou, and thy children, and thy children's children, and thy flocks, and thy herds, and all that thou hast.

And there will I nourish thee.

Genesis 45:1-5, 7-8, 10-11

HUMILITY WILL BE EXALTED

And he put forth a parable to those which were bidden, when he marked how they chose out the chief rooms; saying unto them,

When thou art bidden of any man to a wedding, sit not down in the highest room; lest a more honorable man than thou be bidden of him;

And he that bade thee and him come and say to thee, Give this man place; and thou begin with shame to take the lowest room.

But when thou art bidden, go and sit down in the lowest room; that when he that bade thee cometh, he may say unto thee, Friend, go up higher: then shalt thou have worship in the presence of them that sit at meat with thee.

For whosoever exalteth himself shall be abased; and he that humbleth himself shall be exalted.

Luke 14: 7-11

LAZARUS, COME FORTH

When Jesus therefore saw her weeping which came with her, he groaned in the spirit and was troubled. And said, where have ye laid him? They said unto him, Lord, come and see.
Jesus Wept.   John 11:33-35

Then they took away the stone from the place where the dead was laid. And Jesus lifted up his eyes, and said, Father, I thank thee that thou hast heard me.

And I knew that thou hearest me always: but because of the people which stand by I said it, that they may believe that thou has sent me. And when he thus had spoken, he cried with a loud voice, Lazarus, come forth.

And he that was dead came forth, bound hand and foot with grave clothes: and his face was bound about with a napkin. Jesus said unto them, Loose him, and let him go..

Then many of the Jews which came to Mary, and had seen the things which Jesus did, believed on him. But some of them went their ways to the Pharisees and told them what things Jesus had done.

John 11:41-46

THY GOD MY GOD

And Naomi said, Turn again, my daughters: Why will ye go with me? Are there yet any more sons in my womb, that they may be your husbands?

And they lifted up their voice and wept again: and Orpah kissed her mother in law; but Ruth clave unto her.

And she said, Behold, thy sister in law is gone back unto her people and unto her gods: return thou after thy sister in law.

And Ruth said, Entreat me not to leave thee, or to return from following after thee: for whither thou goest, I will go; and where thou lodgest, I will lodge: thy people shall be my people, and thy God my God:

Where thou diest, will I die, and there will I be buried: the Lord do so to me, and more also, if ought but death part thee and me.

Ruth 1:11, 14-17

Willie James Webb

A NEW HEAVEN AND A NEW EARTH

And I saw a new heaven and a new earth: for the first heaven and the first earth were passed away; and there was no more sea.

And I John saw the holy city, new Jerusalem, coming down from God out of heaven, prepared as a bride adorned for her husband.

And I heard a great voice out of heaven saying, Behold, the tabernacle of God is with men, and he will dwell with them, and they shall be his people, and God himself shall be with them, and be their God.

And God shall wipe away all tears from their eyes; and there shall be no more death, neither sorrow, nor crying, neither shall there be any more pain: for the former things are passed away.

And he that sat upon the throne said, Behold, I make all things new. And he said unto me, write, for these words are true and faithful.

And he said unto me, it is done. I am Alpha and Omega, the beginning and the end. I will give unto him that is a thirst of the fountain of the water of life freely.

He that overcometh shall inherit all things; and I will be his God, and he shall be my son.

Revelation 21:1-7

ONE THING IS NEEDFUL

Now it came to pass, as they went, that he entered into a certain village: and a certain woman named Martha received him into her house.

and she had a sister called Mary, which also sat at Jesus' feet, and heard his word.

But Martha was cumbered about much serving, and came to him, and said, Lord, dost thou not care that my sister hath left me to serve alone? Bid her therefore that she help me.

And Jesus answered and said unto her, Martha, Martha, thou art careful and troubled about many things:

But one thing is needful: and Mary hath chosen that good part, which shall not be taken away from her.

Luke 10:38-42

A REASON TO REJOICE

And the seventy returned again with joy, saying, Lord, even the devils are subject unto us through thy name.

And he said unto them, I beheld Satan as lightning fall from heaven. Behold, I give unto you power to tread on serpents and scorpions, and over all the power of the enemy; and nothing shall be any means hurt you.

Not withstanding in this rejoice not, that the spirits are subject unto your; but rather rejoice, because your names are written in heaven.

In that hour Jesus rejoiced in spirit, and said, I thank thee, O father Lord of heaven and earth, that thou last hid these things from the wise and prudent, and hast revealed them unto babes:

Luke 10:17-21

And he turned him unto his disciples, and said privately, Blessed are the eyes which see the things that ye see:

For I tell you, that many prophets and Kings have desired to see those things which ye see, and have not seen them; and to hear those things which ye hear, and have not heard them.

Luke 10:23-24

GLORYING IN SUFFERING

Seeing that many glory after the flesh, I will glory also.

Are they Hebrews? so am I. Are they Israelites? so am I. Are they the seed of Abraham? so am I.

Are they ministers of Christ?... I am more; in labours more abundant, in stripes above measure, in prisons more frequent, in deaths oft.

Of the Jews five times received I forty stripes save one.

Thrice was I beaten with rods, once was I stoned, thrice I suffered shipwreck, a night and a day I have been in the deep:

In journeyings often, in perils of waters, in perils of robbers, in perils by mine own countrymen, in perils by the heathen, in perils in the city, in perils in the wilderness, in perils in the sea, in perils among false brethren;

In weariness and painfulness, in watchings often, in hunger and thirst, in fastings often, in cold and nakedness.

If I must needs glory, I will glory of the things which concern mine infirmities.

II Corinthians 11: 18, 22-27, 30

GOD HEARS THE CRY OF THE OPPRESSED

And the Lord said, I have surely seen the affliction of my people which are in Egypt, and have heard their cry by reason of their taskmasters; For I know their sorrows:

And I am come down to deliver them out of the hand of the Egyptians, and to bring them up out of that land unto a good land and a large, unto a land flowing with milk and honey; unto the place of the Canaanites, and the Hittites, and the Amorites and the Perizzites, and the Hivites, and the Jebusites.

Now therefore, behold, the cry of the children of Israel is come unto me: and I have also seen the oppression wherewith the Egyptians oppress them.

Come now therefore, and I will send thee unto Pharaoh, that thou mayest bring forth my people the children of Israel out of Egypt.

Exodus 3:7-10

SERVING THE LEAST

Then shall the King say unto them on his right hand, come, ye blessed of my Father, inherit the kingdom prepared for you from the foundation of the world:

For I was an hungered, and ye gave me meat: I was thirsty, and ye gave me drink: I was a stranger, and ye took me in:

Naked, and ye clothed me: I was sick, and ye visited me: I was in prison, and ye came unto me.

Then shall the righteous answer him, saying, Lord, When saw we thee an hungered, and fed thee? or thirsty, and gave thee drink?

When saw we thee a stranger and took thee in? or naked, and clothed thee?

Or when saw we thee sick, or in prison, and came unto thee?

And the King shall answer and say unto them, Verily, I say unto you, in as much as ye have done it unto one of the least of these my brethren, ye have done it to me.

Matthews 25:34-40

Jesus FEEDS THE MULTITUDE

Then Jesus called his disciples unto him, and said, I have compassion on the multitude, because they continue with me now three days, and have nothing to eat: and I will not send them away fasting, lest they faint in the way.

And his disciples say unto him, Whence should we have so much bread in the wilderness, as to fill so great a multitude?

And Jesus saith unto them, how many loaves have ye? And they said, Seven, and a few little fishes.

And he commanded the multitude to sit down on the ground.

And he took the seven loaves and the fishes, and gave thanks, and brake them, and gave to his disciples, and the disciples to the multitude.

And they did all eat, and were filled: and they took up of the broken meat that was left seven baskets full.

And they that did eat were four thousand men, beside women and children.

Matthew 15:32-38

God's Commandment To
PROCLAIM HIS WORDS

Hear, O Israel: The Lord our God is one Lord:

And thou shalt love the Lord thy God with all thine heart, and with all thy soul, and with all thy might.

And these words, which I command thee this day, shall be in thine heart:

And thou shalt teach them diligently unto thy children, and shalt talk of them when thou sittest in thine house, and when thou walkest by the way, and when thou liest down, and when thou risest up.

And thou shalt find them for a sign upon thine hand, and they shall be as frontlets between thine eyes.

And thou shalt write them upon the posts of thy house, and on thy gates.

Deuteronomy 6:4-9

Wisdom and Obedience

My son, forget not my law; but let thine heart keep my commandments:

For length of days, and long life, and peace, shall they add to thee.

Let not mercy and truth forsake thee: bind them about thy neck; Write them upon the table of thine heart:

So shalt thou find favour and good understanding in the sight of God and man.

Trust in the Lord with all thine heart; and lean not unto thine own understanding.

In all thy ways acknowledge Him, and He shall direct thy paths.

Proverbs 3:1-6

Happy is the man that findeth wisdom, and the man that getteth understanding.

Proverbs 3:13

THE GOOD FIGHT

For I am now ready to be offered, and the time of my departure is at hand.

I have fought a good fight, I have finished my course, I have kept the faith:

Henceforth there is laid up for me a crown of righteousness, which the Lord, the righteous judge, shall give me at that day: and not to me only, but unto all them also that love his appearing.

II Timothy 4:6.8

COME FROM AMONG THEM

Be ye not unequally yoked together with unbelievers: for what fellowship hath righteousness with unrighteousness? and what communion hath light with darkness?

And what concord hath Christ with Belial? or what part hath he that believeth with an infidel?

And what agreement hath the temple of God with idols? for ye are the temple of the living God; as God hath said, I will dwell in them, and walk in them; and I will be their God, and they shall be my people.

Wherefore come out from among them, and be ye separate, saith the Lord, and touch not the unclean thing; and I will receive you,

And will be a Father unto you, and ye shall be my sons and daughters, saith the Lord Almighty.

II Corinthians 6:14-18

God's Spiritual Prescriptions
For Healing, Liberation and Salvation

The High Calling and Challenge of Ministry

Giving no offense in anything, that the ministry be not blamed:

But in all things approving ourselves as the ministers of God, in much patience, in afflictions, in necessities, in distresses,

In stripes, in imprisonments, in tumults, in labors, in watchings, in fastings;

By pureness, by knowledge, by long suffering, by kindness, by the Holy Ghost, by love unfeigned,

By the word of truth, by the power of God, by the armor of righteousness on the right hand and on the left,

By honor and dishonor, by evil report and good report: as deceivers, and yet true;

As unknown, and yet well known; as dying, and, behold we live; as chastened, and not killed;

As sorrowful, yet always rejoicing; as poor, yet making many rich; as having nothing, and yet possessing all things.

II Corinthians 6:3-10

A NEW CREATURE IN CHRIST

Therefore if any man be in Christ, he is a new creature: old things are passed away; behold, all things are become new.

And all things are of God, who hath reconciled us to himself by Jesus Christ, and hath given to us the ministry of reconciliation;

To wit that God was in Christ, reconciling the world unto himself, not imputing their trespasses unto them: and hath committed unto us the word of reconciliation.

Now then we are ambassadors for Christ, as though God did beseech you by us: We pray you in Christ's stead, be ye reconciled to God.

For he hath made him to be sin for us, who knew no sin; that we might be made the righteousness of God in him.

II Corinthians 5:17-21

YOU REAP WHAT YOU SOW

Be not deceived: God is not mocked: for whatsoever a man soweth, that shall he also reap.

For he that soweth to his flesh shall of the flesh reap corruption: but he that soweth to the Spirit shall of the spirit reap life everlasting.

And let us not be weary in well doing: for in due season we shall reap, if we faint not.

As we have therefore opportunity, let us do good unto all men, especially unto them who are of the household of faith.

Galatians 6:7-10

A CHOSEN GENERATION

But ye are a chosen generation, a royal priesthood, an holy nation, a peculiar people; that ye should show forth the praises of him who hath called you out of darkness into His marvelous light:

Which in time past were not a people, but are now the people of God:

Which had not obtained mercy, but now have obtained mercy.

I Peter 2:9-10

SEVEN THINGS HATEFUL TO GOD

These six things doth the Lord hate: yea, seven are an abomination unto Him:

A proud look, a lying tongue, and hands that shed innocent blood, An heart that deviseth wicked imaginations, feet that be swift in running to mischief,

A false witness that speaketh lies, and he that soweth discord among brethren.

Proverbs 6:16-19

O JERUSALEM

O Jerusalem, Jerusalem, which killest the prophets, and stonest them

that are sent unto thee; how often would I have gathered thy children together, as a hen doth gather her brood under her wings, and ye would not!

Behold, your house is left unto you desolate: and verily I say unto you, ye shall not see me, until the time come when ye shall say, Blessed is he that cometh in the name of the Lord.

Luke 13:34-35

Time To Awake and Fulfill the Law of Love

Render therefore to all their dues: tribute to whom tribute is due; custom to whom custom; fear to whom fear; honor to whom honor.

Owe no man anything, but to love one another; for he that loveth another hath fulfilled the law.

And that knowing the time, that now it is high time to awake out of sleep: for now is our salvation nearer than when we believed.

The night is for spent, the day is at hand: let us therefore cast off the works of darkness, and let us put on the armour of light.

Romans 13:7-8, 11-12

HOLDFAST TO SOUND DOCTRINE

Preach the word; be instant in season out of season; reprove, rebuke, exhort with all longsuffering and doctrine.

For the time will come when they will not endure sound doctrine; but

after their own lusts shall they heap to themselves teachers, having itching ears;

And they shall turn. away their ears from the truth, and shall be turned unto fables.

But watch thou in all things, endure afflictions, do the work of an evangelist, make full proof of thy ministry.

II Timothy 4:2-5

God Will Exalt The Humble

Humble yourselves therefore under the mighty hand of God, that he may exalt you in due time:

Casting all your care upon him; for he careth for you.

Be sober, be vigilant; because your adversary the devil, as a roaring lion, walketh about, seeking whom he may devour:

I Peter 5:6-8

GOD'S CLEANSING AND PROTECTIVE POWER

For I will take you from among the heathen, and gather you out of all countries, and will bring you into your own land.

Then will I sprinkle clean water upon you, and ye shall be clean: from all your filthiness, and from all your idols, will I cleanse you.

A new heart also will I give you, and a new spirit will I put within you: and I will take away the stony heart out of your flesh, and I will give you a heart of flesh.

And I will put my spirit within you, and cause you to walk in my statutes, and ye shall keep my judgements, and do them.

And ye shall dwell in the land that I gave to your fathers; and ye shall be my people, and I will be your God.

I will save you from all your uncleanliness: and I will call for the corn, and will increase it, and lay no famine upon you.

And I will multiply the fruit of the tree, and the increase of the field, that ye shall receive no more reproach of famine among the heathen.

Ezekiel 36:24-30

BE SOBER CHILDREN OF LIGHT

But ye, brethren, are not in darkness, that that day should overtake you as a thief.

Ye are all the children of light, and the children of the day: We are not of the night, nor of darkness.

Therefore let us not sleep, as do others; but let us watch and be sober.

For they that sleep sleep in the night; and they that be drunken are drunken in the night.

But let us, who are of the day, be sober, putting on the breastplate of faith and love; and for an helmet, the hope of salvation.

I Thessalonians 5:4-8

FOLLOW AFTER RIGHTEOUSNESS

But they that will be rich fall into temptation and a snare, and into many foolish and hurtful lusts, which drown men in destruction and perdition.

For the love of money is the root of all evil: which while some coveted after, they have erred from the faith, and pierced themselves through with many sorrows.

But thou, O man of God, flee these things; and follow after righteousness, godliness, faith, love, patience, meekness.

Fight the good fight of faith, lay hold on eternal life, whereunto thou art also called, and hast professed a good profession before many witnesses.

I Timothy 6:9-12

Be Aware of Deceptions Through Unsound Doctrines

Now I beseech you, brethren, mark them which cause divisions and offenses contrary to the doctrine which ye have learned; and avoid them.

For they that are such serve not our Lord Jesus Christ, but their own belly; and by good words and fair speeches deceive the hearts of the simple.

Romans 16:17-18

DISCERNING THE SPIRIT OF GOD

Beloved, believe not every spirit, but try the spirits whether they are of God: because many false prophets are gone out into the world.

Hereby know ye the Spirit of God: Every spirit that confesseth that Jesus Christ is come in the flesh is of God:

And every spirit that confesseth not that Jesus Christ is come in the flesh is not of God: and this is that spirit of anti-christ, where of ye have heard that it should come; and even now already is it in the world.

Ye are of God, little children, and have overcome them: because greater is he that is in you, than he that is in the world.

I John 4:1-4

THE LAST SUPPER

And as they were eating, Jesus took bread, and blessed it, and brake it, and gave it to the disciples, and said, Take, eat; this is my body.

And he took the cup, and gave thanks, and gave it to them, saying, Drink ye all of it;

For this is my blood of the new testament, which is shed for many for the remission of sins.

But I say unto you, I will not drink henceforth of this fruit of the vine, until that day when I drink it new with you in my Father's Kingdom.

And when they had sung an hymn, they went out into the Mount of Olives.

Matthew 26:26-30

BENEDICTIONS

Now the God of peace, that brought again from the dead our Lord Jesus, that great shepherd of the sheep, through the blood of the everlasting covenant,

Make you perfect in every good work to do his will, working in you that which is well-pleasing in his sight, through Jesus Christ; to whom be glory forever and ever. Amen.

Hebrews 13:20-21

Greet ye one another with a kiss of charity. Peace be with you all that are in Christ Jesus. Amen.

I Peter 5:14

The Lord watch between me and thee, when we are absent one from another.

Genesis 31:49

BENEDICTIONS

The grace of our Lord Jesus Christ be with you all. Amen.

Revelation 22:21

But grow in grace, and in the knowledge of our Lord and Savior Jesus Christ. To him be glory both now and forever. Amen.

II Peters 3:18

Chapter 16

Strategy For The Publication of God's Word

In the publication of God's Word we propose to use science, art and religion. The proper use of science, art and religion is to uplift humanity and to glorify God. Psalm 24 makes the unquestioned declaration, that God owns everything. Genesis confirms that God is the creator. John 1:1 states, "In the beginning was the word, and the word was with God and the Word was God." Therefore, without further elaboration, we can authoritatively conclude, that, it is the duty of science, art and religion to be vehicles in the conveyance of God's word.

In addition to the publication of God's Word in the physical environment this chapter also outlines various ways in which the word can be used to write upon the "tables of the heart." This is a unique resource book of God's Word for Christians, ministers, pastors, counselors, group leaders, musicians, writers, witnesses and publishers of God's Word. This chapter includes many useful ideas as to how the word of God can be used creatively, in our physical and social environment. This book is filled with words of beauty and power, for our eyes to see, our ears to hear and for our hands and hearts to feel.

It is our challenge and sacred duty to publicize God's Word with our hands, our voices and our lives. And God has declared that his word will not return unto him void. The Bible is from God. It is for all nations, all races and all people. It speaks to all humanity. It speaks to each and every person. Its message is personal and corporate. It speaks to you and me, us and them. It is personal, private and public. God's message is local, national and universal. It speaks from eternity, through time, and to eternity. God's Word is Alpha and Omega, the beginning and the end.

This message from God cannot be successfully evaded. No one can legitimately claim that he is above, below or indifferent to this message. No one can legitimately say that, "It is not for me." It does not matter who you are, where you came from, where you are headed, or what your social and economic status may be. *The message is for you.* You may ignore it, deny it, block it or disobey it. You cannot escape the word of God. It will catch you in love or it will catch you in judgment.

> If I ascend up into heaven, thou are there: if I make
> my bed in hell, behold, thou art there.
>
> Psalm 139:8

The moral, social and spiritual decay in our world is at such a critical point that the full strength and potency of God's word must be injected into the mainstream of the American culture and modern civilization. The ideas of this book teaches how to create an environment that teaches the word of God. It contains his salvation message, method and mission to reverse the destructive influences of a secularistic and spiritually degenerating society.

> All scripture is given by inspiration of God, and is profitable for doctrine, for reproof, for correction, for instruction in righteousness.
>
> II Timothy 3:16

This book is based on the premise and promises that God's Word is powerful and transforming within itself. It is based on the premise that the Holy Spirit works through the word to inform, enlighten, educate, guide, inspire, convict, liberate, heal and nurture. But in order for the word to do its sacred work, we must be instruments in the name of God to convey, transcribe, witness and transmit the word to the eyes, ears, minds, hearts and souls of every human being.

Willie James Webb

General Modes for Publicizing God's Word

I. Use art to present God's Word

    1. God's Word can be sculptured
    2. God's Word can be painted
    3. God's Word can be written
    4. God's Word can be chanted
    5. God's Word can be sung
    6. God's Word can be taught
    7. God's Word can be preached
    8. God's Word can be used in ornamental designs
    9. God's Word can be set to music
    10. God's Word can be used to: Inform, warn, petition, persuade, heal, convict, inspire, direct, correct and save.
    11. God's Word can be acted out and dramatized.
    12. God's Word can be lived.

II. God's Word can be used for inscriptions and plaques on the following materials:

    1. Paper
    2. Cloth
    3. leather
    4. Plastics
    5. Wood
    6. Glass
    7. Rubber
    8. Clay
    9. Concrete
    10. Metals
    11. Bricks
    12. Stones

III. God's Word must be inscribed in public and private places.

    1. Homes - The walls, doors, windows, ceilings, skylights, porches, patios, fences, gates, garages and utility structures.

    2. Household items - The furniture, refrigerators, stove, washing machine, dryer and office equipment. Plaques, trophies and certificates.

    3. Churches - Bold outside inscriptions on the roof, walls, windows, doors and parking facility.

    4. Schools, colleges, universities - Inscriptions of wisdom, knowledge, understanding, freedom, law and grace on the outside of buildings, inside of buildings in the corridors, walls, classrooms and restrooms.

    5. Government Buildings -

A. Capitols (Executive Branch) Recommended inscriptions: Knowledge, Wisdom, Understanding, Vision, Guidance, Equality.

B. House of Representatives (Legislative Branch) Recommended inscriptions: Justice, Equality, Freedom, Responsibility, Honesty, Just Laws.

C. Courthouses (Judicial Branch) Recommended inscriptions: Justice, Equality, Righteousness, Freedom, Protection, Mercy, Correction, Education, Counsel.

D. Administration - Service, Respect, Integrity, Dignity

6. Hospitals, prisons and detention facilities - Recommended inscriptions: Wholeness, Healing, Compassion, Correction, Mercy, Grace, Restoration.

7. Bill Boards, statues, plaques and neon signs along expressways, highways and streets - With Biblical inscriptions about the love of God, the light, the hope and the salvation in Jesus Christ.

IV. God's Word must be written on clothing, stationary and office supplies -Headgear, shirts, jackets, stationary, paper, greeting cards, pens, pencils, notebooks and carrying bags.

V. God's word must be written on motor vehicles, automobiles, buses, trucks, trains and planes via paintings, plates, magnetic signs and window inscriptions.

VI. Special Booklets on God's word:

1. Love	15. Knowledge	29. Sound Doctrine
2. Faith	16. Wisdom	30. Truth
3. Hope	17. Understanding	31. Abundant Life
4. Grace	18. Reconciliation	32. Armor of God
5. Justice	19. Prayer	33. Compassion
6. Peace	20. Resurrection	34. Repentance
7. Joy	21. Christmas	35. Justification
8. Freedom	22. Stewardship	36. Spiritual Growth
9. Healing	23. Family	37. Duty of Man
0. Liberation	24. Marriage	38. The Role of Woman
1. Salvation	25. Fellowship	39. Child Rearing
2. Patience	26. Conversion	40. Community
3. Church	27. Government	41. Race
4. Righteousness	28. The Way	42. Light

VII. The utilization of discussion groups to publicize God's Word.

1. Spiritual Groups

      2. Growth Groups
      3. Meditation Groups
      4. Fellowship Groups
      5. Support Groups
      6. Quality Circle Group

VIII. The Worship Serves as a means to publicize God's Word.

      1. Scripture reading
      2. Scripture chanting for children
      3. Scripture chanting for adults
      4. Scripture Highlights
      5. Scripture Recitation
      6. Special Occasion Scripture

IX. Publicize God's Word through music that tells a Biblical story or illustrates a Biblical reference.

      1. Christmas Music
      2. Resurrection Music
      3. Salvation Music
      4. Music on Biblical Personalities
      5. Music on Stories of the Bible
      6. Music on Events of the Bible
      7. Healing Music
      8. Meditation Music

X. Publicize God's Word through simplified Literary means.

      1. Narratives of the Bible.
      2. Children Biblical Books
      3. Flash Cards

Simplified Stories on the following Biblical Characters:

Adam and Eve	Joshua	Nehemiah
Abraham	Jethro	Hosea
Amos	Judas	John The Baptist
Blind Bartimaeus	Lot	Peter
David	Lazarus	Daniel
Mary/Martha	John	Esther
Moses	Ten Lepers	Elijah
Nicodemus	Esau	Paul
Jeremiah	Ezekiel	Sarah
Hebrew Children	Samson	Esau

Hannah	Samuel	Jesus
Saul	Jacob	Solomon
Job	Stephen	Jonathan
Thief on Cross	John the Revelator	Woman at Well
Joseph	Zacchaeus	

The ideas presented in this chapter on the means and methods of publicizing God's Word are not exhaustive. They are meant to give general ideas about some of the means and methods of presenting God's Word. God's Word offers an endless array of innovative and creative means and methods of presentations and illustrations. Hopefully, this book will stimulate religion, art and science in making the Word of God a concrete reality in our culture, our hearts and minds.

About the Author

The author has spent the greater portion of his life being intimately involved in studying and living in the human conflicts and cultural crisis of our time. In his search for answers he has earned a B.A. degree from Morehouse College, a M.A. degree from Atlanta University, a M.S. degree from Georgia State University and a Master of Divinity degree from the Interdenominational Theological Center in Atlanta, Georgia. Additionally, he has over twenty-five years of continuing education at various educational institutions, including the University of Georgia. He is a certified addiction counselor and criminal justice specialist. He has over thirty years of experience as a mental health and criminal justice professional, pastoral counselor, a Christian minlister, pastor and educator. He has worked the full gamut of social services, remediation, sustenance, prevention and growth. He has worked effectively with unruly, neglected and delinquent children, dysfunctional families, clients in mental health, criminal justice, geriatrics and the homeless. The author has designed, established, and directed social service programs in correctional institutions as well as in the community. He has done extensive social research and has written two masters theses in regards to juvenile recidivism and management of community based social service programs. He is the author of ***Psychotrauma***

Webb was born in Macon County, Alabama where he graduated from Tuskegee Institute High School as the president of his senior class, on the campus where Booker T. Washington founded Tuskegee Institute in 1881. He graduated from Morehouse College as the most outstanding student in religion. He was licensed and ordained to preach at Macedonia Baptist Church, his home church in Notasulga, Alabama. While in Atlanta, Georgia he served over twenty years as assistant pastor and later as interim pastor of the historic Wheat Street Baptist Church. He is the founder and pastor of Foundation Baptist Church in Atlanta.

The author is currecntly an adjunct professor of theology at the Interdenominational Theological Center (ITC) through its Continuing Education Program. Through the Certificate in Theology Program at ITC, Webb hopes to provide theological exposure to many pastors, ministers and lay persons who for various reasons do not go to seminary, but can benefit significantly from education in theology.

The author is convinced by his long years of intense life experiences and top level academic and professional exposures that ONLY THE WORD OF GOD IS SUFFICIENT TO SAVE HUMANITY AND HUMAN CULTURE FROM SELF-DESTRUCTION. This book is designed to make God's Word plain and to stimulate true religion, art and science in making the Word of God a concrete reality in the social and physical environment, human culture, human hearts, minds and spirits.

Printed in the United States
768100001B